Charles Jackson

A Vindication of the Marquis of Dalhousie's Indian Administration

Charles Jackson

A Vindication of the Marquis of Dalhousie's Indian Administration

ISBN/EAN: 9783337061555

Printed in Europe, USA, Canada, Australia, Japan

Cover: Foto ©ninafisch / pixelio.de

More available books at **www.hansebooks.com**

A

VINDICATION

OF THE

MARQUIS OF DALHOUSIE

INDIAN ADMINISTRATION.

BY

SIR CHARLES JACKSON.

CONTENTS.

INTRODUCTION.

Several works have lately appeared containing reflections on the Indian Administration of the late Marquis of Dalhousie. According to Mr. Kaye, that statesman was a 'great minute writer,' 'with unrivalled powers of special pleading,'[1] who committed many unwise and unjust acts, which caused general discontent, and contributed to produce the Sepoy war. Mr. Arnold represents Lord Dalhousie as an able administrator and statesman, driven by 'one dominant passion' 'to 'the very verge of conventional justice, generosity, 'and good faith, and even sometimes not a little

---

[1] Kaye's *Sepoy War*, pp. 73-78.

' beyond those boundaries,'[1] and the narrative of his annexations seems ' doubtless more like counting ' out the spoil of brigands in a wood than detailing ' the acts of English statesmanship;'[2] and Major Bell affirms that Lord Dalhousie ' lowered the reputation ' of our Government by repeated breaches of our ' pledged faith,' and adds, in words for which he claims additional weight as being ' carefully chosen,' that ' he was the very worst and basest of rulers.'[3]

I shall not comment on the language in which some of these opinions are conveyed, although I think a life devoted to his country, and prematurely worn out in its service, might have secured for Lord Dalhousie at least the semblance of respect. But without pausing to enter into any verbal controversy, I propose, in a short explanation and defence of his policy, to examine whether there is any just foundation for such an estimate of his character and administration. I think that such an inquiry, impartially

---

[1] ARNOLD's *Dalhousie Administration*, p. 200.

[2] ARNOLD, p. 199.

[3] *The Empire in India*, by Major BELL, p. 26.

conducted, will show that Lord Dalhousie was a great administrator and statesman, with large views as to the requirements of India and his own duties as its Governor-General; that his policy was the policy of progress and civilization; and that his measures added materially to the happiness and prosperity of the people of India.

I do not propose to write a history of Lord Dalhousie's administration. I shall pass over in silence his annexation of the Punjaub, and shall not repeat the praises, which have been well bestowed, on his admirable arrangements, and selection of officers, for the government of that province. I shall not speak of the conquest of Pegu, nor dwell on his judicious arrangements on that occasion, which I had particular opportunities of observing. Neither is it my intention to chronicle those peaceful glories, which throw a brighter light on his administration than all his conquests and annexations, his canals, railroads, electric telegraph, and other public works, as well as his anna postage. I shall

not describe his vigilant superintendence of every
department of the State,—how he swept away useless
Boards, substituting in their stead individual responsibility,—how he selected meritorious officers for his
work, as it were by instinct,—how firmly he punished,
—how gracefully he praised.   It would be agreeable
indeed to speak of all these things ; but my principal object, at present, is the more limited purpose
of vindicating his policy and reputation from the
attacks of his assailants.

ANNEXATIONS BY LAPSE.

I WILL first consider the annexations of the States of Sattarah, Nagpore, Jhansi, and Sumbulpore.

When a Hindoo has no male issue, he generally adopts the child of some relation as his own son. The son thus adopted is as capable as a real son of performing the religious ceremonies which are supposed to be of special benefit to the soul of a deceased Hindoo, and is therefore entitled to all the rights of a real son in the property of his adopting father. This general rule is, however, subject to one exception or qualification. When the Hindoo is a prince, holding his principality subordinate to, or as a gift from a paramount state, it is a condition of succession to the principality that the adoption be made with the consent of such paramount state. His private property will pass to the adopted son, whether the paramount state has or has not consented to the adoption ; but, in the absence of such consent, the principality reverts to the paramount state.

Sattarah and Jhansi were incorporated into our dominions under the operation of the last rule. The Rajahs of those dependent principalities[1] died without male issue of their bodies, but each of them

---

[1] We took the first Rajah of Sattarah from the prison of the Peishwa, and elevated him to the throne, as the Sattarah treaty recites, ' in consideration of the antiquity of ' his family. The treaty provided that the Rajah should hold his dominions ' in ' subordinate co-operation with ' the British Government, and be guided in all matters by the advice of the Resident ; that he should not increase or diminish his military establishment without our consent ; and that all his intercourse with other courts, even the negotiations for the marriages of his family, should be conducted through the Resident.

Jhansi was a Soubahdaree under the Peishwa, whose rights were transferred to the British by conquest. By treaty the Indian Government ' consented on certain conditions to constitute Rao ' Ramchund the hereditary chief,' not on the ground of hereditary right, but ' in consideration of the character of ' his grandfather, and in deference to the wish of that relative. We afterwards conferred the title of Rajah on the Soubahdar. Colonel Low, who opposed the other annexations, assented to this, on the ground that the Rajah was a subject rather than a prince.

adopted a son a short time before his death, without
receiving permission to do so from the paramount
power, the British Government. Nagpore and
Sumbulpore were annexed because their last Rajahs,
also dependent princes,[1] died without heirs. No
adoption was made by either of these Rajahs, and
their states reverted to the British Government,
the paramount power which created them. In all
these cases Lord Dalhousie declined to waive the
right which had accrued to the Government. He
refused to reconstitute these lapsed dynasties, or to
give away the lapsed territories a second time to an
aged lady and boys, who were proposed to him as
candidates for the vacant thrones. His decision,
on each of these cases of lapse, received the
support of the Court of Directors and the Board
of Control.

It is erroneous to suppose that this doctrine of

---

[1] The British Government acquired Nagpore by conquest in
1818, and conferred it on its first and last Rajah, who paid a
tribute of 80,000l. a year. Sumbulpore was ceded to the British
Government by the Nagpore state in 1817 and 1826, and conferred
by the British Government on its first Rajah, as Mr. Kaye informs
us, ' under terms which would have warranted the resumption of
' the state on the death of the first incumbent; but twice the
' sovereign rights had been bestowed anew upon members of the
' family.'

lapse violated the religious feelings of the people
with respect to adoption. Mr. Kaye observes:—
' Ere long there was a word which came to be more
' dreaded than that of conquest. The native mind
' is readily convinced by the inexorable logic of the
' sword. There are, however, manifest compensa-
' tions; his religion is not invaded, his institutions
' are not violated, but LAPSE is a dreadful and
' appalling word, for it pursues the victim beyond
' the grave. Its significance in his eyes is nothing
' short of eternal condemnation.'[1] I confess to a
want of faith in the existence of this feeling of dread;
but if it was felt, there was no foundation for it.
Lord Dalhousie never disputed the validity of these
adoptions as such. He never denied their alleged
spiritual effect, and nothing he said or did could
affect their validity as acts done in the performance
of a religious duty. He recognized them as facts,
and was careful to give effect to them so far as the
private property of these princes was concerned.
In the Jhansi case, when the Resident proposed
that all the property of the late Rajah should be
given to his Ranee, Lord Dalhousie objected that it

---

[1] KAYE, p. 69.

was 'beyond the power of the Government so to
' dispose of the property of the Rajah, which by law
' will belong to the son whom he adopted. The
' adoption was good for the conveyance of private
' rights, though not for the transfer of the prin-
' cipality.'

One would suppose, from the way in which Lord
Dalhousie has been assailed, that this 'dreadful
' and appalling' doctrine of lapse was first suggested
and enforced by him; but it was the settled public
law of India, repeatedly acted on by the Indian
Government, and sanctioned by the Court of Directors, long before he landed in that country.

The law which requires the sanction of Government for the adoption of a son is applicable to all
persons holding tenures under Government, such as
Jaghiredars,[1] Wuttundars, and Enamdars,[2] as well
as dependent princes. The state revenues are
alienated in all these cases, and the permission of
the paramount state is necessary to continue to an
adopted son such alienations of revenue. Under
these circumstances, and considering the extent to
which revenue free grants had prevailed, this law

---

[1] *The Empire in India*, by Major BELL, p. 147.
[2] STEELE's *Laws and Customs*, p. 185.

could not have been a novelty, but must, on the contrary, have been well known throughout India.

To avoid wearying our readers with a legal dissertation on this question, we will cite a Minute of Sir George Clerk's on the Sattarah annexation. Sir George deservedly holds a high rank among Indian statesmen, and his authority is considered, by the opponents of Lord Dalhousie's policy, to be of great weight. He opposed the annexation of Sattarah, yet felt compelled to admit that ' the sanction of ' the paramount state is by custom required to ' render an adoption to a principality valid. In the ' time of our predecessors this was a source of profit ' to the treasury.' That the principle of this law was well known and established throughout India, appears from the answers of the Residents at the different native Courts to an inquiry made by the Government of Bombay. These answers establish that in all parts of India, with the exception of one petty state, 'the previous recognition of the ruler was necessary to give the adopted son a title to grants of revenue, or privileges emanating from the state.[1]

---

[1] See *Report* of Mr. W. Hart, Bombay Civil Service, dated March 27, 1847. Mr. Kaye in his work admits the law to be as we have stated it (see p. 70).

That this law was acted upon by the British Government before Lord Dalhousie's time is also clear. In 1831, the Bombay Government resolved to ' continue to grant or to withhold its permission to ' adopt according to circumstances.' In 1834, the Court of Directors ordered, 'wherever it is optional ' with you to give or to withhold your consent to ' adoptions, the indulgence should be the excep- ' tion, not the rule, and should never be granted ' but as a special mark of favour and approbation.'[1] In 1835, Rao Ram Chund, the dependent Rajah of Jhansi, died, leaving two uncles, and a boy adopted the day before his death, without the permission of the British Government. The Government of India, without inquiry into the fact of adoption, and treating it as an immaterial circumstance, appointed the elder of the two uncles Rajah ; and on his death without issue, in 1838, they placed the younger uncle on the throne, although the adopted son was still living, and asserted his claim.[2] In 1841, permission to

---

[1] Mr. WILLOUGHBY's *Minute* in the Sattarah papers.

[2] See *Memorandum* of Mr. Secretary (now Sir J. P.) Grant, and the *Minute* of Lord Dalhousie in the Jhansi papers.

adopt was refused to the state of Angria Colaba, which consequently lapsed.   On that occasion the Indian Government, composed of Lord Auckland, Mr. Bird, and Mr. Prinsep, declared their intention 'to persevere in the one clear and ' direct course of abandoning no just and honour- ' able accession of territory or revenue, while all ' existing claims of right are at the same time ' scrupulously respected.'   Again, in 1843, in consequence of a refusal to permit adoption, the small state of Mandvee also lapsed, and became incorporated into the British dominions.[1]

It has been suggested that permission to adopt should always be given on payment of a nuzzur (present).   But this suggestion is not applicable to these lapses, for it is a fact that the permission of Government was not asked by any of the Rajahs whose territories lapsed, except the Rajah of Sattarah; and his application, if it ever left his palace before his death, of which there is no evidence in the papers, was made too late to reach

---

[1] See Mr. WILLOUGHBY's *Minute* on the Sattarah question, 14th of May, 1848.   Lord Dalhousie called this *Minute* ' a text-book on adoption,' and he was in the habit of referring to it when similar questions subsequently arose.

the Government in his lifetime.[1]   It is said that
Lord Dalhousie would have refused permission
if it had been asked; but that is mere conjecture,
and I am considering the facts that happened,
and not what might have occurred.   But if Lord
Dalhousie had been afforded an opportunity of
granting or refusing permission to adopt, I do not
think he would have been bound to consent on
payment of a nuzzur.   No authority can be produced in support of such a doctrine.   Major Bell
in his work admits that such permission was sometimes refused by the native governments in the
case of Jaghires,[2] and the Jaghires of Nopanee,
Chinchoree, Sonee, and others in the Deccan and
South Mahratta country, were all incorporated into
our dominions in consequence of similar refusals
by the British Government.[3]   I have also shown
that applications for leave to adopt were refused by
governments that preceded Lord Dalhousie's.   The
law has always been stated in an unqualified way,
and the fact that permission must be obtained

---

[1] It was sealed on the evening of the 3rd of April, 1848,
and the Rajah died at half-past one, P.M., of the 5th of April.

[2] *The Empire in India*, by Major BELL, p. 147.

[3] Mr. WILLOUGHBY's *Minute*, Sattarah case, 14th of May, 1848.

implies that it may be refused; otherwise the permission is unnecessary and a farce. The exaction of a nuzzur, however, invests the application with all the appearance of a stern reality; for it is difficult to perceive the difference in principle between a right to demand a present, undefined in its amount, and which might (as was proposed in the Nagpore case) amount to 120,000*l.* a year increased tribute to the paramount power, and a right to refuse permission to adopt. If the nuzzur required was not paid, the paramount power would not consent to the adoption.

Sir George Clerk, in his Minute on the Sattarah annexation, raised an objection, which, if valid, would also apply to the lapse of Jhansi and Nagpore. His objection is founded on the language of the treaty, conferring Sattarah on the first Rajah 'and his heirs and successors.' Sir George Clerk, although he admits 'that the ' sanction of the paramount state is by custom ' required to render the adoption to a principality ' valid,' nevertheless contends that such sanction could not be refused without injustice, as the grant was in perpetual sovereignty to the Rajah, 'his ' heirs and successors,' and that the adopted son was such heir and successor, as he stood in the same relation as a real son. But this argument is inconsistent with the previous admission, and assumes the whole question in dispute ; for if the consent of the paramount state is necessary to render an adopted son capable of inheriting a principality, and the Rajah of Sattarah did not obtain such consent, then the son adopted by him was not his heir or successor within the meaning of the treaty. It can scarcely be contended, that the words ' heirs and successors ' in the treaty, meant those who were not heirs or successors according to the law applicable to the subject.

The dynasties of all these dependent princes became extinct on their deaths. The adopted sons of the Rajahs of Sattarah and Jhansi could not inherit, because the permission of the paramount power was not obtained for their adoption, and there was no other heir to those sovereignties. The Rajah of Nagpore left no heir in the male line (and no other heir could inherit[1]), and neither

---

[1] See Sir R. JENKINS' *Report on Nagpore*, in which he states the principles regulating the succession to the throne. He says,

he nor his widow complicated the question by adopting a son. The Rajah of Sumbulpore obtained his sovereignty from the British Government under a treaty which did not constitute him an hereditary prince.[1] Under these different circumstances, all these dependent thrones were vacant, and, as the sovereignty must be in some one, they reverted to the British Government, the paramount power which had created the expired dynasties. This is the 'appalling' doctrine of lapse, and it is worth while to observe how little Lord Dalhousie had to do with it. He did not invent it. He did not refuse these princes permission to adopt. He merely happened to be the governor of a country in which these lapses occurred by operation of law.

But then it is said, although the Rajah of Sattarah and Jhansi did not obtain permission to adopt, the Government should have recognized their adopted sons; and although the Rajah of Nagpore never adopted a son, and his Ranees neither adopted

'It is hereditary in the entire male line from the common ancestor 'or first founder of the dynasty, to the exclusion of females or 'their issue.'

[1] See KAYE's *Sepoy War*, p. 97.

nor expressed any intention of doing so, the Government should have required the Ranees to adopt, or called upon the principal men of the province to select some person as their prince.[1] These suggestions raise the real question. If Lord Dalhousie is open to censure, it cannot be for lapses of territory which were effected by operation of law, but it must be because he did not waive the rights which the law gave him, and reconstitute, and in fact recreate, these lapsed and extinct dynasties. This is the real issue on which Lord Dalhousie has himself put these annexations. In his Sattarah Minute he said:—' I ' do not presume to dispute the wisdom of creating ' the Raj of Sattarah. I conceive that the same ' reasons do not prevail for its reconstitution now, ' when it is again placed by events at our disposal.' [2] In his Nagpore Minute, he says:—' The simple ' question for determination is, whether the sove- ' reignty of Nagpore, which was bestowed as a gift ' upon a Goojur by the British Government in 1818, ' should now be conferred upon somebody else as a ' gift a second time.'

---

[1] See Colonel Low's *Minute on the Nagpore Annexation.*

[2] In another part of the same Minute he says, " While I find ' no sufficient reason for the reconstitution of Sattarah," &c.

2

Lord Dalhousie decided that it would not be for the benefit of the British Government, or the good of the native population, to reconstitute these dependent states. I think no statesman, with any sense of his responsibility, could arrive at any other conclusion.

The continuance of these dependent states could not have been beneficial to the British Government. They were the creations of their policy in former times, and the objects for which they were created had long ceased to exist. Some of them were established that they might act as " counterpoises " to other states, but these latter states had since dwindled into comparative insignificance, and no longer required a counterpoise. Others were set up because it was thought their creation would be popular, and they would act as safety valves, affording employment to the turbulent soldiery then roving over the Deccan; but the power of the Mahrattas had since been broken, and their predatory troops were no longer feared. The dislike of the Court of Directors, in those days, to the extension of their territory, and the difficulty experienced in administering such rapidly increasing dominions, were also reasons for the creation of these states, but when

Lord Dalhousie governed India, they were situated in the midst of our territory; their annexation consolidated our dominions without increasing our frontier ; and their administration was scarcely a perceptible tax on our increased resources.

These dependent sovereignties might have been convenient at the time of their creation, but they were the fruitful source of subsequent trouble. Their sovereigns either rebelled against us, or so mismanaged their territory and oppressed their subjects, that we were obliged to interfere. We were compelled to dethrone and exile the first Rajah of Sattarah. Jhansi was so misgoverned by its first two Rajahs, that its revenues fell from 180,000l. a year to 30,000l. a year ; and at last we were obliged to assume the management of the province. The state of Jaloun, in 1840, was thus described by Lord Auckland :—' In the course of nine or ten years, ' the land had been most profusely alienated ; debts ' to the amount of 30 lacs had been contracted; ' extensive districts had been mortgaged as a security ' for them ; there was neither order nor security in ' the territory; every village was exposed to the ' attacks of plunderers; cultivation was deserted ; ' and a country which had been fruitful and pros-

'perous, was from day to day becoming deso-
'late.'   In Mysore, the incapacity and oppressive conduct of its Rajah compelled us to deprive
him of the administration of his country, and for
many years we have governed it for him. Sumbulpore was grievously misgoverned. In Nagpore, the
Rajah being an infant, and the Regent, Banka Baee,
a female, we were obliged to administer the government during the minority. What became of that
country after it was handed over to the Rajah on
his coming of age, I will show hereafter.

One of these states, Sattarah, interfered with
our military communications, being situated between
the stations of Poona and Belgaum, and all these
states, when annexed, were either entirely, or in
a great degree, surrounded by British territory.
The existence of native states so situated, must have
been a source of weakness rather than strength.
India is not so exceptional a country that common
sense cannot be applied to its political questions,
and if a foreign state and jurisdiction would be
deemed an intolerable annoyance in the midst of
a European kingdom, it cannot be considered a
benefit in the centre of our Asiatic dominions.

But the benefit of these dependent states to

the British Government was not the sole question for Lord Dalhousie's consideration. His mind would have found little satisfaction in such a narrow and selfish view of the subject. His Minutes show that he anxiously weighed the consequences to the inhabitants of these territories if he reconstituted their extinct dynasties, and that he formed a deliberate opinion that the British rule was better than that of any native ruler, and certainly much better than could be expected from the rule of the aged lady and boys he was asked to place on the vacant thrones. In his Nagpore Minute, Lord Dalhousie observed, ' I place the ' interests of the people of Nagpore foremost among ' the considerations which induce me to advise that ' that state should now pass under British govern- ' ment; for I conscientiously declare that unless ' I believed that the prosperity and happiness of ' its inhabitants would be promoted by their being ' placed permanently under British rule, no other ' advantages which could arise out of the measure ' would move me to propose it.' In his Sattarah Minute, when speaking of the benefits to be derived from incorporating that territory into the British dominions, he says, ' In my conscience I believe

' we should ensure to the population of the state
' a perpetuity of that just and mild government
' which they have lately enjoyed, but which they
' will hold by a poor and uncertain tenure, indeed,
' if we resolve now to continue the raj, and deliver
' it over to a boy brought up in obscurity, selected
' for adoption almost by chance, and of whose
' character and qualities nothing whatever was
' known by the Rajah who adopted him, nothing
' whatever is known to us.'

The character and fitness of the candidates for
the vacant thrones was another grave question
involved in the reconstitution of these extinct dynasties. The Rajahs of Sattarah and Jhansi each
adopted distant relatives, who were mere boys.
The Ranee Banka Baee, who had been Regent
during the minority of the late Rajah, and was
seventy-five years old, was proposed by the Resident
as the future Sovereign of Nagpore; and in case the
Government should object to her, he suggested that
a youth named Jeswunt Rao, a relative of the late
Rajah on the female side, who was described as
tractable but not brilliant, should be selected as
Rajah; and if he should be objected to, the Resident
proposed that another relative on the female side,

of whom he did not speak so favourably, a boy named Appa Sahib, should be placed on the throne. The Ranees of the late Rajah made no suggestion to the Government, and were probably well content with the intentions of the Resident in favour of the Ranee Banka Bace.[1] The question, therefore, for Lord Dalhousie's decision was not merely whether he should reconstitute these lapsed dynasties, but whether he should reconstitute them in favour of an aged lady tottering on the brink of the grave, who from her age, sex, and Asiatic custom, would be dependent on those around her, or in favour of a minor whose disposition and talents were un-known, and whose minority would in itself produce

---

[1] This old Ranee, who was much respected, and had great influence in the palace, expressed a hope to the Resident ' that ' the interests of the Bhonsla family would continue to be inter-' woven with the Berar kingdom,' an observation which, in the absence of any adoption or intention to adopt, probably expressed her own claim to consideration. The other Ranees were probably at that time under the influence of Banka Bace. After the decision of Government in favour of annexation, and, according to Mr. Temple's Report, after the death of the senior widow at the close of the year 1855, the Ranees adopted Appa Sahib, and of course antedated his adoption, but the report of the Resident, who was in communication with the Ranees after the Rajah's death, and a petition of Banka Bace's, were conclusive, and Lord Canning refused to acknowledge Appa Sahib as the adopted son of the Rajah.

all the evils of an Asiatic regency. Now the only
chance an Indian prince has of becoming fit for
his position is that he should be brought up in
adversity, like the Rajah of Sattarah, or that he
should fight his way up to the throne, in which
case, however, though fit to rule in one sense,
he is generally a tyrant. But what hope could
be entertained of any Indian prince brought up
in the purple—of his becoming anything but an
indolent, sensual, and tyrannical sovereign? To
show what a ruler one of these Indian princes
was, who was brought up under the eye of Sir
Richard Jenkins, and who, Mr. Kaye assures us,
was not the worst specimen of his class, we will
here extract from a Report of Mr. Mansell, the
Resident at Nagpore, a description of the last ruler
of that country.[1]

'A distaste for business and low habits seem
' the distinguishing features of his temperament.
' Any strict attention to affairs of state paid by
' him has been enforced by the remonstrance of
' the Resident, while his natural inclination has
' again led him, when unchecked, to absorb him-

---

[1] Report of Mr. Mansell, dated 14th December, 1853. Parliamentary Papers relating to the Rajah of Berar, p. 13.

' self in the society of low followers, in the sports
' of wrestling, kite-flying, and cards, in singing and
' dancing, and in the intercourse of his dancing-
' girls. A saying of his to an officer who, about
' a year ago, was appointed to the office of Durbar
' Vakeel, on the removal of the old incumbent,
' will not incorrectly illustrate his character. The
' audience of investiture was over, and the new
' Vakeel was then dismissed with these words :
' " Now, go away, and study the provisions of
' " the treaty, so as to see that they are enforced,
' " to protect me in the enjoyment of those plea-
' " sures of dancing and singing that I have loved
' " from my boyhood." '

' A concubine, by name Janee, is spoken of as
' having led the Rajah into confirmed habits of
' drinking about eight years since, so that now, when
' not ill, his drinking exceeds a bottle of brandy a
' day. Not a few disgraceful scenes have occurred
' at the palace while the Rajah has been overcome
' with spirits, and generally it may be said that
' indisposition has thus grown into incapacity to
' discharge business, in the thoughtful and earnest
' form becoming a sovereign, for any continuance
' of time.' . . . .

'The addiction to the low pleasures of the
'harem was always a marked characteristic of the
'Rajah, and has become more baneful since the
'habit of drinking has so grown upon him. His
'time is now absorbed in the paltry conversation
'and the mean pursuits of the concubines, and he
'now with reluctance leaves the inner apartments.
'The Vakeel has frequently had to coerce the Rajah
'by very decided language into coming into court,
'and disposing of such business as required to be
'done in a public form.'   .   .   .   .

'When thus the Rajah has been divesting him-
'self of much of the best part of his character, he
'has been acquiring habits of avarice that have led
'him into a systematic indifference to the claims of
'the administration of justice, and to the selection
'of merit in making official appointments. Of late
'years all the anxiety of the Rajah and of his
'favourite ministers has been to feed the privy
'purse by an annual income of two or more lacs of
'rupees from nuzzurs, fines, bribes, confiscation of
'property of deceased estates, the composition of
'public defaulters, or the sale of their effects, and
'such like sources. The Rajah has thus been led
'on by his avarice to discard all feeling, and to

' throw himself into the hands of the most unprin-
' cipled of his servants, who plundered the country,
' and put justice up to sale for profits but a slender
' part of which reached the Rajah.   He has done
' many cruel acts, and even carried war into the
' country of his feudal dependants, on the misre-
' presentation of those parties, gilded by the offer
' of a nuzzur.   Orders of the most contradictory
' character have been issued at the bid of rival
' parties from time to time in cases before the
' law courts, the number of which is notorious.   As
' soon as indifference and a blind submission to
' the advice of certain evil advisers became profit-
' able, the Rajah just contented himself with sign-
' ing and sealing the proceedings that awarded a
' decision to the best paymaster.   All this has
' aggravated the low tone of mind originally belong-
' ing to the Rajah.   He acts and thinks like a
' village chandler.   Profits and pickings are to be
' made anyhow.   The choicest amusement of the
' Rajah is an auction sale, when some unfortunate
' widow is ruled not to be entitled to her husband's
' estate, or when some public defaulter is found
' to have made away with revenue collections, just
' equal to the sum he paid five or six years before

' for his situation of revenue collector to the
' Rajah.' . . . .

  ' The favourable features in the condition of the
' country are mainly those that existed when the
' state was entrusted to the Rajah in 1830, and
' the unfavourable ones are mainly those that the
' country has assumed under the Rajah's rule. That
' the partial pleasing aspect of things is not over-
' shadowed or destroyed, is mainly owing to the
' occasional interference of the Resident, who, when
' affairs had become particularly gloomy, caused a
' better tone to be infused into every department,
' and secured a new lease of decency to be succeeded
' by the old degradation under a new incumbent of
' the Residency. The machinery that has mainly
' kept society together under the latter part of the
' Rajah's reign, has been the almost British discipline
' of the troops bequeathed by the transfer of 1830
' to the Rajah. This has made him all-powerful,
' capable equally of setting an enemy and justice at
' defiance. The revenue system of fixed leases left
' behind by Mr. Jenkins has, on the other hand,
' preserved the finances of the state, and the agri-
' cultural interest, from being sacrificed wholly to
' reckless folly or temporary expedients to raise funds.'

Mr. Kaye's work furnishes us with another graphic description of native rulers. Speaking of the successive kings of Oude, he writes :—

'It would take long to trace the history of the
'progressive misrule of the Oude dominions under a
'succession of sovereigns all of the same class—
'passive permitters of evil rather than active
'perpetrators of iniquity, careless of, but not rejoic-
'ing in, the sufferings of their people. The rulers
'of Oude, whether Wuzeers or kings, had not the
'energy to be tyrants. They simply allowed things
'to take their course. Sunk in voluptuousness
'and pollution, often too horribly revolting to be
'described, they gave themselves up to the guidance
'of panders and parasites, and cared not so long
'as these wretched creatures administered to their
'sensual appetites. Affairs of state were pushed
'aside as painful intrusions. Corruption stalked
'openly abroad, every one had his price ; place,
'honour, justice—everything was to be bought ;
'fiddlers and barbers, pimps and mountebanks,
'became great functionaries. There were high
'revels at the capital, whilst, in the interior of
'the country, every kind of enormity was being
'exercised to wring from the helpless people the

'money which supplied the indulgences of the
'court. Much of the land was farmed out to large
'contractors, who exacted every possible farthing
'from the cultivators, and were not seldom, upon
'complaint of extortion, made, unless inquiry
'were silenced by corruption, to disgorge into the
'royal treasury a portion of their gains. Murders
'of the most revolting type, gang robberies of the
'most outrageous character, were committed in open
'day. There were no courts of justice except at
'Lucknow; no police but at the capital and on the
'frontier. The British troops were continually
'called out to coerce refractory landowners, and to
'stimulate revenue collection at the point of the
'bayonet. The sovereign—Wuzeer or king—knew
'that they would do their duty; knew that, under
'the obligations of the treaty, his authority would
'be supported; and so he lay secure in his Zenana,
'and fiddled whilst his country was in flames.'

The arguments in favour of perpetuating these
lapsed states, are to be found in the Minutes of Sir
George Clerk and Colonel Low, the chief opponents
of Lord Dalhousie's policy, who contended that
dependent states were useful, inasmuch as they

afforded employment to a native nobility and turbulent spirits who would not be employed by us, and who would sink into ' the dead level ' of the population under our rule ; that other native states would be alarmed by these annexations, fearing the application of the same doctrines to their own successions ; that our territory was already large enough ; and that natives prefer their own rulers to the British Government.

The first of these arguments may be true in fact, and yet entitled to very little consideration. I think it probable that few of the nobility of these courts would be employed by a well-ordered government, and certainly the turbulent spirits, who lived by intrigue and violence, would find their occupation gone. But the eye of the statesman, who considered this question, did not dwell upon the particular interests of a noble class or a turbulent soldiery, but on the wider claims of the great mass of the population. The nobles and soldiers attached to these courts were pensioned,[1] and, with the

---

[1] On the lapse of all these territories, Lord Dalhousie provided ample means for the Ranees and ladies of the deceased Rajahs, and also pensions for the officers and adherents of the family, as well as six months' pay for the troops.

natural advantages of their birth and position, might well be left to fight their own battle. If the native noble is worth preserving, he can preserve himself and his own position under our rule, as the Maharajah of Burdwan and others have done. At all events, Lord Dalhousie was not the man to give away a kingdom to support a nobility and soldiery, whether they were or were not ' turbulent spirits.' All his Minutes on these annexations show, that his mind dwelt much on the misgovernment of native states, and the greater happiness the mass of the people would experience under our rule.[1] And surely this was a far nobler object to keep in view than the conciliation and employment of native nobles,—a class very well able to take care of themselves, and not generally eulogized by those who are brought into contact with them.

Then it is suggested that all the Princes of India were alarmed by these annexations, and feared the application of the doctrine of lapse to their own successions; but the truth is, that the doctrine was

---

[1] See extracts already given, and his observations on the government of Jaloun and Jhansi, in his *Minute on the Jhansi Annexation.*

capable of a very limited application among Princes. Lord Dalhousie repeatedly declared that it was applicable to dependent states only. Speaking of his own Minute on the Sattarah annexation, he observed, ' The opinion which I gave was restricted ' wholly to subordinate states, to those dependent ' principalities which either as the virtual creation ' of the British Government, or from their former ' position, stood in such relation to that Government ' as gave to it the recognized right of a paramount ' power in all questions of the adoption of an heir ' to the sovereignty of that state. The opinion I ' gave referred exclusively to " subordinate states," ' to a " dependent principality," like that of Sat- ' tarah and others that have been named.'[1] I do not believe that one independent sovereign was alarmed by these lapses of territory, but if there

---

[1] *Minute* of Lord Dalhousie on *the Nagpore Annexation,* dated 28th January, 1854—p. 35 of the Nagpore papers. Unfortunately in all printed copies of Lord Dalhousie's *Minute on the Sattarah annexation,* in one of the most important passages, the word ' independent ' appears instead of ' dependent.' I know not how it is written in the original, but the whole argument of the Minute requires that it should be ' dependent.' See this passage set out in Mr. Kaye's work, p. 74.

was such a sovereign, his fear was most unreason-
able, and might have been removed by ten minutes'
conversation with the Resident at his Court, or a
reference to Calcutta.   But the range of this supposed dread was still more limited, for the doctrine,
requiring the consent of the British Government to
adoptions by dependent sovereigns, is inapplicable to
those of the Mahomedan faith, and it was Lord
Dalhousie's fate to gather in nearly the whole crop
of dependent *Hindoo* territories.   I believe that
Mysore was the only one remaining at the close of
his administration.

Then it is said that these annexations enlarged
our territory, which was already quite large enough.
That they enlarged our territory is a geographical
fact, which cannot be disputed, but the question
is, whether these annexations unduly taxed our
resources, or diminished our strength.   With respect
to Sattarah, Lord Dalhousie observed, 'There may
' be conflict of opinion as to the advantage or pro-
' priety of extending our already vast possessions
' beyond their present limits.   No man can more
' sincerely deprecate than I do any extension of
' the frontiers of our territory which can be avoided,
' or which may not become indispensably necessary

' from considerations of our own safety, and of the
' maintenance of the tranquillity of our provinces.
' But I cannot conceive it possible for any one to
' dispute the policy of taking advantage of every
' just opportunity which presents itself *for consoli-*
' *dating* the territories that already belong to us, by
' taking possession of states which may lapse *in the*
' *midst of them;* for thus getting rid of these paltry
' intervening principalities, which may be made a
' means of annoyance, but which can never, I
' venture to think, be a source of strength.' . . . .
' It would be difficult to imagine a case to which the
' rule founded on this general principle would be
' more closely applicable than the Raj of Sattarah.
' The territories lie in the very heart of our pos-
' sessions.   They are interposed between the two
' principal military stations in the Presidency of
' Bombay, and are at least calculated, in the hands
' of an independent sovereign, to form an obstacle
' to safe communication and combined military
' movements. The district is fertile, and the revenue
' productive.   By incorporating Sattarah with our
' possessions we should acquire continuity of mili-
' tary communication, and increase the revenues of
' the state.'   On the lapse of Jhansi, Lord Dal-

housie wrote, ' The British Government will not
' derive any material advantage from the possession
' of this territory, for it is of no great extent, and the
' revenue is inconsiderable, but it lies in the midst
' of other British districts, and the possession of it
' as our own will tend to the improvement of the
' general internal administration of our possessions
' in Bundelkund.' Sumbulpore, when it lapsed in
1855, was situated between our provinces of Nagpore
and Cuttack, and was in fact surrounded by British
territory. The position of Nagpore is thus described
by Lord Dalhousie :—' Its incorporation, however,
' with the British empire, would extinguish a
' government having separate feelings and interests,
' and would absorb a separate military power out of
' which there must always be a possibility that
' embarrassment, if not anxiety, might some day
' arise. The incorporation of Nagpore would give
' to us a territory which comprises 80,000 square
' miles, producing an annual revenue of 40 lacs of
' rupees, and containing more than 4,000,000 of
' people who have long desired to return to our rule.
' It would completely surround with British terri-
' tory the dominions of his Highness the Nizam, in
' a manner highly beneficial for the purposes of

' internal administration. It would render con-
' tinuous several British provinces, between which
' foreign territory is now interposed. Orissa in the
' east, would be joined with Candeish in the west,
' and Berar, recently assigned to the south, would
' be made fully continuous with the Saugor and
' Nerbudda territories to the north. It would place
' the only direct line of communication which exists
' between Calcutta and Bombay almost within
' British territory, whereas the road now passes for
' a considerable distance through foreign states.'
. . . . ' To sum up all in one sentence, the
' possession of Nagpore would combine our military
' strength, would enlarge our commercial resources,
' and would materially tend to consolidate our
' power.'

The observation, that the natives of India prefer
the rule of their own princes to that of our Government, did not apply to the inhabitants of Nagpore.
They had experienced the benefits of our rule
when Sir R. Jenkins governed the country, during
the minority of the late Rajah, and they afterwards
suffered under that Rajah from a system of
government which has been already described,
and the consequence was, that they were anxious to

revert to our rule.[1] Whether this preference for
rulers of their own colour and race, animated the
inhabitants of the other lapsed states at the time of
their annexation, it is difficult to say, but if it did,
they only entertained a feeling common to a large
mass of our Indian population, and all subjugated
races, and 'if it be the duty of a Governor-General to
defer to such a feeling, we must be prepared to
go further, and leave India to its native princes.
If Lord Dalhousie was not right in assuming
that our Government was the very best the natives
could get, and in treating any alleged preference
of theirs for native rulers as immaterial; if he
ought, in deference to the supposed wishes of the
people, to have declined the government of these
lapsed states, and recreated these extinct dynasties,
how could he justify his retention of any other
province of our Indian dominions? Why should
he, in deference to such a preference, relinquish
provinces acquired by law, and in defiance of such
a preference, retain other provinces? Our present

---

[1] See the *Report* of Mr. Mansell, the Resident at the time
of the lapse, and the *Minutes* of Colonel Low and Sir F. Halliday
in the Parliamentary papers relating to the Rajah of Berar, pp. 21,
47 note, and 52.

right to remain in India is not based on any love of the natives for our rule, or any preference for our government, and we shall only involve ourselves in difficulties, if we either act or argue on such an assumption.

Lastly, it is said that these annexations caused general discontent, and were a principal cause of the rebellion of 1857. But if this were so, how was it that Nagpore and Sattarah remained faithful to our rule? Surely the inhabitants of Sattarah had as much cause of complaint as those of Jhansi, and Nagpore as Sumbulpore, and yet during the rebellion neither Nagpore nor Sattarah joined the insurgents. It was no fear of British troops that caused the difference, for the European regiment had long been withdrawn from Nagpore, and Sattarah never had such a garrison. When states, supposed to be suffering under a common wrong, act so differently, it is probable that the alleged wrong had nothing to do with their conduct, which must be explained in some other way. It is true that Jhansi and Sumbulpore were carried away by the storm wave of rebellion, which rose so high in 1857, but is there any evidence to show that their rebellion was caused by annexation ? As they did rebel, it is assumed that their annexation was the cause, but let us suppose that Lord Dalhousie had reconstituted Sumbulpore and Jhansi. Will any one who knows India venture to assert, that, under such circumstances, the new Princes would have remained faithful to us in 1857 ? Would a native Prince have secured Sumbulpore, with its almost barbarous people, from the contagion and wild excitement of rebellion ? Is it to be believed that when Central India rose against us, Jhansi would have remained faithful, if we had acknowledged the adoption by the last Rajah ? If Holkar and Scindiah experienced such difficulty in steering through that storm, is it to be supposed that a mere boy at Jhansi would have been able to do so ?

What would have been said of Lord Dalhousie, if Nagpore, with its vast cotton-fields, were now under a native sovereign, indifferent to our commercial interests and incapable of furthering them ? Would not Lord Dalhousie have been assailed as a short-sighted politician, who lost a golden opportunity of acquiring a country capable of yielding large supplies of the great staple of our manufactures? But no one who has read his Minute on the annexation of Nagpore, can dispute his qualifications for such a charge as India. In the fifty-second paragraph, he says, 'The possession ' of Nagpore will materially aid in supplying a ' want, upon the secure supply of which much of ' the manufacturing prosperity of England depends. ' Many items go to make up the sum of that pro- ' sperity; but there is perhaps no one item in it ' all upon which more depends than upon a steady ' and full supply of the staple article of cotton ' wool. The importance of this question is ever ' pressing itself upon all who are connected with ' the administration of either England or India.' . . . . 'I need hardly say then that my attention ' has never ceased to be directed to the means ' of obtaining those cheap and abundant fields of ' supply, and that ready access to them, which ' alone can release England from almost total ' dependence upon a foreign power, for the supply ' of an absolutely indispensable material of her ' trade.'

From what has been said of these annexations, I think it sufficiently appears that Lord Dalhousie

did not originate the doctrine of lapse; that he
did not extend it, by applying it in a manner in
which it was never before applied; and that his
application of it to these states, was not forced
upon a reluctant government at home, but was
fully sanctioned in each case. I have endeavoured
to show, that these states lapsed by operation of law;
that Lord Dalhousie carefully considered the question of their reconstitution; that weighty reasons
support the conclusions to which he came; and that
these annexations were injurious neither to the inhabitants of the territories annexed, nor to the
interests of the British empire. And if I have
succeeded in showing this, it is not easy to see upon
what ground, the imputations, which have been so
freely cast upon the memory of a great statesman,
are to be justified.

The question as to these annexations is one
of great moment, for if Lord Dalhousie acted unjustly, we have as yet acquired no title by effluxion
of time, and, even now, it is our duty to make
restitution, and reconstitute these states. It would
be strange morality, indeed, to abuse Lord Dalhousie for his annexations, and yet hold fast the
territories he acquired. Is the India Office now

prepared to reconstitute these dynasties, and relinquish the revenue arising from these states?
If not,—if Lord Dalhousie's policy is to be upheld
in fact,—surely it would be as well to abstain from
casting reflections and doubt upon it, and thus
exciting hopes in India, which must end in dis-
appointment.

KEROWLEE.

THE little Rajpoot State of Kerowlee escaped annexation, but still Lord Dalhousie is blamed by Mr. Kaye because he ventured to think it might be annexed, and, entertaining doubts about it, referred the question to the Court of Directors, thus causing a delay which alarmed the Rajpoot States.

The Rajah of Kerowlee died in July, 1852, after adopting a boy, named Bhurt Pal, without the sanction of the British Government. Two questions arose for decision : first, whether Kerowlee was a dependent state; second, whether it was politic to annex it.

No one reading Mr. Kaye's narrative would suppose that there had been any question as to the independence of this state, but Lord Dalhousie asserted that by the third article of the treaty our supremacy was ' specifically admitted,' and that for many years the government had been administered by our officers. The Court of Directors differed from Lord Dalhousie, and thought that Kerowlee was only a protected ally, but they did not produce the treaty when the papers were called for by the House of Commons.

Although Lord Dalhousie thought the doctrine of lapse might be applied to Kerowlee, yet it is clear, from his language and conduct, that he entertained great doubts as to the policy of annexing this Rajpoot State. All the merit of entertaining these doubts is ascribed by Mr. Kaye to Sir F. Currie, and Lord Dalhousie's vision is described as clouded ' by the film of a foregone conclusion.'[1] ' To a man,' Mr. Kaye observes, ' who ' had graduated from boyhood upwards in Indian ' statesmanship' (Sir F. Currie), ' there was some- ' thing almost sacrilegious in the idea of laying ' a destroying hand even upon the least of the ' ancient houses of Rajpootana—of destroying titles

---

[1] KAYE's *Sepoy War*, p..98.

'that had been honoured long years before the face
'of the white man had been seen in the country.
'But impressions of this kind are the growth of
'long intercourse with the people themselves, and
'we cannot be surprised that after a year or two
'of Indian government, Lord Dalhousie, with all
'his unrivalled quickness of perception, should not
'have thoroughly understood the vital differences
'between the various races inhabiting the great
'continent of India.'[1] This seems to be written
in support of 'a foregone conclusion,' that nothing
Lord Dalhousie said or did could be right, for it
is clear from the papers, that Lord Dalhousie was
the first to suggest these 'vital differences.' In his
Minute, written before Sir F. Currie's, he states
the very objection Mr. Kaye supposes he could
not appreciate. 'On the other hand,' he says,
'the state is isolated, and would not consolidate
'our territories as in the case of Sattarah. Though
'not a very old state, still it is a Rajpoot princi-
'pality, and, unlike the existing Mahratta and
'Mahomedan dynasties, has the claim of antiquity
'in its favour. The refusal of sanction to adoption

---

[1] KAYE'S *Sepoy War*, p. 93.

' in the case of Kerowlee might create alarm and
' dissatisfaction in the older and more powerful
' states in Rajpootana, as being apparently signi-
' ficant of the intention of the British Government
' towards themselves. Such an alarm would be
' unfounded. For I presume that the Government
' of India would not at any time be disposed to
' interfere with the customary modes of suc-
' cession among these old Rajpoot states, whose
' antiquity, whose position, and feelings would all
' make it our policy to leave them in the possession
' of such independence as they now enjoy. But
' although the alarm would be unfounded, it may
' possibly be considered undesirable to run any risk
' of exciting it, by refusing to allow the adoption in
' Kerowlee.' . . . . ' The arguments appear to me
' to preponderate in favour of causing Kerowlee to
' lapse, but as the Honourable Court may desire to
' continue the succession on the ground of its being
' a Rajpoot state, I do not propose to refuse at once
' the sanction of the Government to the adoption,
' but to refer it to the Court of Directors, *soliciting*
' *an immediate reply.*'

The papers left India in September, 1852, but
the answer of the Court of Directors did not reach

Calcutta till March, 1853. For this delay Lord Dalhousie was not responsible, but nothing could have been more fortunate than its occurrence, for it turned out that Bhurt Pal, the alleged adopted son, had no title to the succession, and that the claims of one Mudden Pal were supported by all the influential persons in the state. If Lord Dalhousie had blindly followed the Resident's suggestion, and recognized the adoption of Bhurt Pal, he would have done wrong, and caused discontent.

When the letter of the Court of Directors, recognizing the adoption of Bhurt Pal, arrived in India, Lord Dalhousie proceeded calmly to inquire into the rival claims. He observed:—' I do not antici- ' pate any sort of disturbance in Kerowlee from delay ' in deciding the case. If there were, I should still ' pursue these investigations, for it would be better ' to risk tumult than to give a wrongful decision on ' the succession to a throne.' But when, with the concurrence of Sir H. Lawrence, he had made up his mind in favour of Mudden Pal, he took the responsibility of immediate recognition on himself, and without further reference to the Court of Directors, (who had decided in favour of Bhurt Pal,) issued his orders recognizing Mudden Pal as Rajah.

This act saved much time, but brought on him a severe rebuke from the Court of Directors.

I know not on what authority Mr. Kaye suggests that, during the period of two years occupied by these investigations, the houses of Rajpootana were kept in suspense, and that it was well known the British Government was discussing the policy of annexing Kerowlee,[1] for there could have been no secret or suspense as to the annexation, after the receipt of the despatch of the Court of Directors. If the effect of that letter was not well known in Kerowlee, as I believe it was, soon after it reached India, the fact that the Government was taking pains to investigate the rights of the rival claimants, and to ascertain the feelings of the people respecting them, must have satisfied every one, that the question before the British Government was not annexation, but succession,—not the destruction of the dynasty, but its continuance.

Then Mr. Kaye observes : ' It was not strange ' indeed that *a year or two* afterwards there should ' have been in circulation *all over the country* ominous ' reports to the effect that the policy of Lord Dal-

---

[1] KAYE's *Sepoy War*, p. 96.

' housie had eventually triumphed, and that the
' gradual absorption of all the Rajpoot states had
' been sanctioned by the Home Government.'[1]
A little more particularity as to the date and
venue of this rumour, would have shown to what
extent it was connected with the proposed annexation of Kerowlee. It is very improbable that a
native rumour would be couched in the exact language used by Mr. Kaye, and a little alteration in
its terms would merely convey the prevalent notion
in India, that we intend to absorb the whole country.
But whatever the rumour may have been, it was,
like most Indian rumours, totally destitute of truth.

---

[1] KAYE'S *Sepoy War*, p. 97.

NANA SAHIB'S CLAIMS.

I HAVE had some difficulty in making out the precise charge brought against Lord Dalhousie, with respect to the claims of the notorious Nana Sahib to succeed to the pension and jaghire of his adoptive father, the ex-Peishwa. Mr. Kaye speaks of ' the ' harshness of the sentence,'[1] and cites, with manifest approbation, a memorial of the Nana Sahib to the Court of Directors, in which his most impudent claim is certainly argued with some ingenuity ; but Mr. Kaye does not show in what respect Lord Dalhousie erred, or what injustice was done to the Nana. His narrative omits every fact which would

---

[1] KAYE'S *Sepoy War*, 103.

4—2

show the audacity of the claim, and states every
unsupported argument as if worthy of belief, and
he may intend to point the moral of the tale when
he relates the sad events at Cawnpore.   Mr.
Arnold says,[1] that ' firm to the course of losing no
' chance of economy or sequestration, Lord Dal-
' housie rejected his claim,' and he adds : ' It is
' enough to say he was an adopted Hindoo son ; he
' claimed the city and pension by right of adoption ;
' the first was prolonged to him for a time, the last
' was refused to him altogether, and Cawnpore told
' in 1857 how a Hindoo prince's heart regarded
' Lord Dalhousie's doctrine of expedient escheats.'
These are insinuations rather than charges, but
whether they are one or the other, what becomes of
them when it is shown, that the decision of Nana
Sahib's claim raised no question whatever either
of adoption or escheat ?   Lord Dalhousie's decision
would have been the same if the Nana had been
a real, instead of an adopted, son ; and his opinion
that the pension of Bajee Rao was, what it professed
to be, a-pension for his life, and not a grant in
perpetuity of 80,000l. a year to him and his heirs,

---

[1] ARNOLD'S *Dalhousie Administration*, pp. 127 and 128.

excluded all occasion for raising any question of
' expedient escheat,' even if there had been a disposition to do so, which I believe to be a perfectly
unfounded suggestion.

In 1818, the Peishwa Bajee Rao, having been
defeated by the British forces, entered into negotiations with Sir John Malcolm, then the Governor-
General's agent in the Deccan. The terms eventually agreed on, were, that Bajee Rao should resign
all sovereign power, and leave the Deccan, and
that he should ' receive a liberal pension from the
' Company's Government for the support of himself
' and family;' Sir John Malcolm engaging that
it should not be less than eight lacs of rupees
(80,000*l.*) per annum. This arrangement with the
Peishwa was confirmed by the Government, although
they disapproved of the terms, and considered the
pension much too large. Subsequently, the Government, probably adverting to the terms of the
arrangement, which contemplated the pension of
80,000*l.* a year as the least sum which Bajee Rao
should receive, granted him a tract of land near
Bithoor as a jaghire, during pleasure; with a
limited civil and criminal jurisdiction over its

inhabitants.[1] I shall afterwards show that there is
no pretence for saying that it was contemplated by
any of the parties that this should be a pension
and jaghire in perpetuity, more than any other
ordinary pension granted by the Government should
be in perpetuity.

Bajee Rao subsequently adopted two sons, one
of whom was the noted Dhoondoo Punt Nana Sahib,
and often pressed upon the Government the propriety of making a future provision for his family.[2]
The very fact of such an application, to say nothing
of its terms, implies that the ex-Peishwa himself
understood that his pension was granted for his
life only. If it were certain that the pension was
hereditary, he would have been silent; if there
had been any well-founded grounds for contending
that it was hereditary, he would have asserted those
grounds. I do not find that he ever went so far as
to ask for a continuance of the pension and jaghire
to his heirs. No assurance of the continuance

---

[1] See *Regulation* I. of 1832, and particularly the Preamble.

[2] *Minute* of Court of Directors, 6th November, 1844 ; Letter
of Colonel Manson, 6th November, 1847 ; *Report* of Colonel
Manson of 10th February, 1851, paragraph 3.

of it was ever given him, and he accumulated large property, probably with the purpose of making that provision for his descendants, which he had no reason to believe the Government would make. He died in January, 1851, leaving a will in favour of Nana Sahib, who accordingly took possession of all the personal property which Bajee Rao had thus accumulated. What this amounted to no one knows. Nana Sahib admitted it to be 280,000*l.*; but both the Lieutenant-Governor and Lord Dalhousie believed that this admission fell far short of the truth, and it is not likely that the truth would be told by him pending the claim then made on the Government.

The first petition presented on behalf of the Nana, after the ex-Peishwa's death, contains a vague request that Nana Sahib, his widowed mother, his younger brother, his sisters and cousins, as well as his old servants, might 'be supported as ' hitherto.' This comparatively modest application was subsequently, on the 29th of July, 1851, improved upon, and the Nana, having in the interval probably been advised that the pension might be mistaken for an inheritance, made the bolder demand for a continuance of the pension and jaghire in favour of himself, *and* that a provision suited to the rank of the late ex-Peishwa might be granted to him. The claim first came before Mr. Thomason, the Lieutenant-Governor of the North-West Provinces, who treated it as an application for some portion of the pension,[1] which he decidedly refused. The Lieutenant-Governor, however, proposed, that the land contained in the Bithoor jaghire should be allowed to continue free of land-tax during the life of the Nana, provided he continued to reside there.

The papers then came before Lord Dalhousie, who observed:[2]—'For thirty-three years the Peishwa 'received an annual clear stipend of 80,000*l.*, 'besides the proceeds of the jaghire. In that 'time he received the enormous sum of more than

---

[1] See commencement of the letter of Secretary to Government of the North-West Provinces to Sir H. Elliot, 13th September, 1851. There is probably a mistranslation, and the claim for a provision in the Nana's petition was probably put in the alternative, ' or that a provision,' &c.

[2] The extract is from a letter of Sir H. Elliot, Secretary to the Government of India, to the Governor of the North-West Provinces, dated 24th September, 1851. It contains internal evidence that it is a *Minute* of Lord Dalhousie's, cast into the form of a letter, according to the practice at that time.

' two millions and a half sterling. He had no
' charges to maintain, he has left no sons of his
' own, and has bequeathed property to the amount
' of twenty-eight lacs to his family. Those who
' remain have no claim whatever on the considera-
' tion of the Government. Neither have they any
' claim on its charity, because the income left to
' them is amply sufficient. Even if it were not
' ample, the Peishwa, out of his vast resources, ought,
' his lordship observed, to have made it so, and
' the probability is, that the property left is in
' reality much larger than it is avowed to be.'

Lord Dalhousie did not, however, interfere with
the Lieutenant-Governor's arrangement as to the
Bithoor jaghire, which remained in the Nana's
possession rent-free, that is to say, free from payment of land-tax. This was an act of favour for
which Nana Sahib should have been grateful, as
the Preamble of Regulation I. of 1832 proves, that
the jaghire was resumable by the Government at
pleasure.[1]

---

[1] I have been unable to ascertain the value of the jaghire.
It appears from the correspondence, that Bajee Rao expended
large sums in buildings on the estate, and I hear that many of his
old followers resided on the land.

Lord Dalhousie's expression that the Peishwa 'left no sons of his own,' may have been unfortunate, inasmuch as it may afford a ground, however slight, for the argument of Mr. Arnold, that the non-continuance of the ex-Peishwa's pension was a fresh application of the doctrine of escheat, founded on a refusal to recognize the adoption of Nana Sahib.   But the whole correspondence shows that this is not the fact; that the real issue was whether the pension was hereditary or for life only; and that Lord Dalhousie, in adverting to the failure of Bajee Rao's natural heirs, was using an argument *à fortiori*, which was in truth unnecessary to his conclusion.

It was not till after this decision that the claim of the Nana assumed the distinct form of a claim of right to succeed to the pension.   His memorial to the Court of Directors relied on the terms of the arrangement, entered into between Sir John Malcolm and Bajee Rao, granting a pension to the latter ' for ' the support of himself and family,' and insisted that such provision indicated the hereditary character of the grant, as it was unnecessary and unmeaning in its application to a mere life grant, ' for a provision ' for the support of a prince necessarily included 'the maintenance of his family.'[1] The Court of Directors regarded the pension as they would any other pension granted to their dependants for the maintenance of themselves and their families, and held that the pension was not hereditary, and that Nana Sahib had no claim whatever to its continuance.

The fourth article of the agreement entered into between Sir John Malcolm and Bajee Rao, provided, 'that Bajee Rao shall, on his voluntarily agreeing 'to this arrangement, receive a liberal pension from 'the Company's Government for the support of 'himself and family,' and the amount was thus defined ; 'Brigadier General Malcolm takes upon 'himself to engage that it shall not be less than 'eight lacs of rupees per annum.' The memorial contended that this fourth article amounted to a perpetual charge on the revenues in favour of Bajee Rao and his heirs. But the word 'pension' does not necessarily import an hereditary pension, and, on the contrary, its ordinary and popular meaning is an annuity payable for the life of the recipient. Here the grantee of the pension is Bajee Rao alone,

---

[1] KAYE's *Sepoy War*, p. 105.

and not Bajee Rao and his heirs. The construction
contended for must therefore rest on the words
' for the support of himself and his family.' But
these are not the words ordinarily used in treaties,
or other formal documents, to indicate the hereditary
character of a grant; and if it was intended to
confer an hereditary grant, there was no difficulty
in expressing that intention in language that would
obviate all doubt. It is obvious that the words are
capable of receiving the interpretation that the
pension was intended to provide for the support not
only of the ex-Peishwa, but of his family also. It is
objected that on this hypothesis the words would
be superfluous and unmeaning; but I demur to the
statement that a provision for a prince necessarily
includes the maintenance of his family. Those
words are expressive in two senses,—first, as in-
timating the intention of the Government that the
pension should be large enough to provide for the
family of the Peishwa as well as for himself,—and
secondly, as expressing that it was designed to throw
the burden of the family on the ex-Peishwa himself,
and prevent applications for pensions from his relations, such as the Government afterwards received
from numerous retainers of Bajee Rao, (not included

in the term 'family,') and felt compelled to grant.

Assuming, however, that these words are ambiguous, let us consider, for that is the best criterion of their meaning, what was the understanding concerning them of both parties to the original arrangement, as evidenced by their declarations and acts.

It is clear that Sir John Malcolm only intended to grant a pension for life. His letter of the 19th of June, 1818, points out that if Bajee Rao had protracted the contest, many men 'would have 'rejoined his army, and if that should have occurred, 'there would have been the necessity of our bringing 'into the field armies which would have cost more '*than the value of the life pension granted to Bajee Rao.*'[1] And it is remarkable that Mr. Kaye himself, in another work, takes this accurate view of the case. In his *Life of Sir John Malcolm* he calls Bajee Rao 'an annuitant,' and argues on the assumption that the pension ceased with his life.[2]

Again, what evidence is there that Bajee Rao

---

[1] KAYE's *Life of Sir J. Malcolm*, vol. ii., p. 259.
[2] *Ibid.* p. 265.

understood that the pension was granted for anything
more than his life ?   I have already adverted to his
applications for a provision for his family after his
death.   All were appeals to the generosity of the
Government for future favour, not claims of right
founded on an interpretation, however erroneous, of
the agreement with Sir J. Malcolm.   Is it to be
supposed that if the ex-Peishwa had not himself
understood that his pension was for life, his application would have assumed that form?   Surely
he would either have remained silent concerning a
pension which he thought assured to his successors
without question; or he would have asked for the
recognition of his adopted son as the future successor
to his pension ; or, if he supposed that the hereditary
character of the pension was unfairly in controversy,
he would have put forward his own construction of
the treaty, and claimed the performance of what he
understood to be its obligations.

Again, if the continuance of this pension was
matter of contract, or understood so to be, there
seems to have been nothing to prevent the Nana
Sahib from suing the Government for the payment
of it.   No question of personal dignity interfered
with his adoption of that course, if he had been

so advised, for he and his father' allowed a lady
of their family, the widow of Chinna Appa, a
younger brother of Bajee Rao, to institute a suit
against the Government, and they furnished the
funds for its prosecution. No question of jurisdiction prevented his application to the courts of
justice. There does not seem to be any substantial difference between his claim, and that which
has been notoriously carried through all the Courts
in a suit between the late Mr. Dyce Sombre or his
representatives, and the East India Company.

I trust I have shown that Lord Dalhousie was
right in protecting the public purse from this
preposterous demand. If a moderate degree of
liberality towards native grandees be reasonable
and politic, the continuance of the jaghire was
a sufficient compliance with such a policy. If the
proper refusal of a larger claim engendered hatred,
no blame can attach to Lord Dalhousie.

I have dwelt upon this question longer than I
think is warranted by its importance ; for, of all
the imputations cast upon Lord Dalhousie's memory
by his assailants, this, of a supposed grievance of
the Nana Sahib, has ever seemed to me to be
the least substantial. Those who will take the

trouble fairly to investigate the question, can hardly fail to come to the conclusion, that it is only by the exercise of a perverse ingenuity that British writers can find, in the dealings of Lord Dalhousie's government with this monster of treachery and cruelty, any explanation—I suppose they would hardly account it, extenuation—of the foulest crime of the Indian Mutiny.

ACT XI. OF 1852.

I AGREE with Mr. Kaye in considering the resumption measures of the Indian Government most
oppressive. But they were not the work of Lord
Dalhousie, or the result of his policy. These
resumptions were recommended by the first revenue
authorities in India, sanctioned by the Court of
Directors, and carried out with ruthless energy in
Bengal, Behar, the North-West Provinces, and
Bombay, long before Lord Dalhousie landed. All
that can be laid to Lord Dalhousie's charge, is,
that he assented to a resumption Act for certain
districts in Bombay,[1] which was a mere supplement

---

[1] Act XI. of 1852.

to previous legislation, and was less oppressive than former enactments on the same subject.

Under the old native governments, it was the practice to grant lands free from revenue (or land-tax), in favour of religious persons or communities, and as rewards for public and other services[1] rendered to the state or its sovereign. As the tax on land was the principal source of revenue, the existence of large tracts of land exempted from its payment, of necessity, either caused a great loss to the Government, or the increased taxation of the unexempted lands. An inquiry into the validity of these revenue-free tenures, on first taking possession of a province, was a wise measure; but the old resumption Regulations applied to provinces long under our rule, and subjected to investigation the titles of persons who had held land for long periods, without paying revenue. They were framed on the principle that there was a general liability on all landowners to pay the tax, and cast the *onus* of proving exemption on the

---

[1] Some of these services were not of a reputable, or even a decent nature.

landowners, many of whom had lost the evidences of it. These Regulations disregarded the presumptions arising from lapse of time, and the conduct of the Government in never compelling payment of the tax, and made the landowner prove his own case affirmatively, irrespective of those presumptions.[1]

Act IX. of 1852 was prepared by the Government of Bombay, and forwarded to Calcutta. I was then acting as fourth, or law, member of the Council, and entertained strong objections to the Act; but feeling the hopelessness of attempting to subvert a policy already established, I objected to the severity of some of its clauses, rather than its principle. These objections were overruled by the civilian members, one of whom, I remember, considered my views ' occidental rather than Oriental.' When the Act came before the Council, Lord Dalhousie expressed a verbal opinion in its favour, but the ground of that opinion I do not remember.[2]

---

[1] See Bengal Regulations XIV. of 1825. The previous Bombay Regulations were XVII. of 1827, chapters 9 and 10, and Regulation VI. of 1833.

[2] I do not recollect seeing any Minute of Lord Dalhousie's on the subject.

Being overruled, and disapproving of the Act, I took
no further interest in it, and it passed the Council,
without any material alteration in its very untech-
nical language.

Although I agree with Mr. Kaye in much that
he has said of resumption measures, I think that,
misled by Mr. Seton Karr's memorial, he has given
an exaggerated account of the working of this Act.
Mr. Seton Karr is quoted as saying:—' Each day
' produced its list of victims, and the good fortune
' of those who escaped but added to the pangs of
' the crowd who came forth from the shearing-house
' shorn to the skin, unable to work, ashamed to
' beg, condemned to penury.' And Mr. Kaye
adds,—' the titles of no less than 35,000 estates,
' great and small, were called for by the Commission,
' and during the first five years of its operations,
' three-fifths of them were confiscated.'[1] Now,
most readers would suppose from these statements,
that these enamdars were immediately turned out of
their houses and lands, and reduced to penury.
But, in fact, there was no ousting from possession,
the object of these investigations being a resump-

---

[1] KAYE's *Sepoy War*, p. 177.

tion of the right to the land revenue, and not a resumption of the land itself. The title which was set aside was not the title to land, but the title to hold it free from the payment of revenue. It is true, that in the case of a pretended village enamdar, that is, the holder of a whole estate let out to subholders, resumption became the same as dispossession, because its consequence was, that the actual holder of each field came to pay the assessment of his land direct to Government, nothing being then paid to the quasi enamdar. But then, in all these cases, the Act of 1852 permitted,[1] and the Commissioners always allowed, unless it was a case of gross fraud,[2] the person claiming as enamdar, whose title was disproved, to retain the privileges of enamdar during his life. In this respect, this much-abused Act of 1852, was more lenient in its provisions than the kindred enactments of the Bengal Presidency.

The Enam Commissioners were, in another respect, much more lenient than other resumption

---

[1] Act XI. of 1852, schedule B., rule vi., and its provisions, and rule vii., provision 7.

[2] *Ex relatione* W. Hart, Esq., formerly Chief Enam Commissioner.

authorities.[1] Previous to the institution of that Commission, it was the universal custom, in all investigations of the titles of alleged enams, to throw the burden of proving his title upon the landowner. But in 1845, it was settled by the Enam Commission, that the *onus probandi* was on the Government, and this principle was not departed from by Act XI. of 1852, which recognizes titles with no other foundation than long exemption from payment of revenue.[2]

I shall not dwell further on this resumption measure, for it must be clear to every unprejudiced mind, that it formed no part of Lord Dalhousie's policy, and that the oppressive nature of the Act has been greatly exaggerated. It had nothing to

---

[1] For a full account of these resumption operations in Bombay, see a printed letter, dated 25th July, 1859, addressed by W. Hart, Esq., formerly Chief Enam Commissioner, to W. Ewart, Esq., Chairman of the Committee appointed to inquire into the prospects of European colonization and settlement in India. This letter shows, that the Act was less oppressive in its provisions than the former rules under which the Commission acted.

[2] See sections xi. and xii. of Mr. Hart's letter to Mr. Ewart, before referred to, pp. 6, 7, and 8 ; and Act XI. of 1852, schedule B., rules iii. and iv., and provision 5 of rule vii., and provision 4 of rule viii.

do with the subsequent outbreak in a part of the Southern Mahratta country, and there was no rebellion in the other districts in which Act XI. of 1852 was put in force, notwithstanding the excitement occasioned by a mutiny at Kholapore, and intrigues at Sattarah.

SPOLIATION OF THE NAGPORE PALACE—
THE BHONSLA FUND.

———◆———

MR. KAYE complains of 'the spoliation of the
'palace, which followed closely upon the extinction
'of the Raj' of Nagpore.[1] He speaks of the sale
of the live and dead stock, of the furniture removed,
and of the jewels sent to the Calcutta market, as
creating a worse impression than the seizure of
the kingdom itself. He also observes, 'I know
'that the question of public and private property
'is a difficult one, and I shall not attempt to
'decide it here. I only speak of the intense
'mortification that these sales create in the family
'itself, and the bad impression which they produce
'throughout the country. Rightly or wrongly,

---

[1] KAYE's *Sepoy War*, p. 83.

' they cast great discredit on our name; and *the*
' *gain of money* is not worth the loss of character.'[1]
Mr. Arnold also speaks of this transaction, as if
Lord Dalhousie had confiscated the property of
the late Rajah.[2]

But Lord Dalhousie did not sell this property
as public property of the Nagpore State, to which
the British Government became entitled on their
accession to the sovereignty. The difficult questions referred to by Mr. Kaye,—whether the property of an absolute monarch is not all public
property, and whether it is possible to distinguish
between the public and private property of such a
sovereign—though referred to, were not actually
relied on, until Lord Canning's government seized
the property appertaining to the Raj of Tanjore.
Lord Dalhousie did not claim this property for
the British Government, or confiscate it, but he
directed its realization by sale, with the view of
protecting the proceeds from misappropriation.
In his Minute of the 10th of June, 1854, he
observed :—[3]

[1] KAYE's *Sepoy War*, p. 84, note.
[2] ARNOLD's *Dalhousie Administration*, vol. ii. p. 166.
[3] Parl. Papers relating to Annexation of Berar, 1856, p. 10.

'*It is not, I think, desirable that the property*
' which the Honourable Court has considered to
' be "fairly at the disposal of the Government,"
' *should be alienated from the family*, but neither
' should it be given up, to be appropriated and
' squandered by the Ranees.

'I would, therefore, propose that *jewels, and
' furniture, and other personal property suitable to their
' rank, having been allotted to the Ranees*, the value
' of the *rest* of the jewels, &c., should be realized,
' and that the proceeds should be constituted a
' fund *for the benefit of the Bhonsla family*. As the
' Commissioner seems to think that the value likely
' to be realized has been over-estimated, the Govern-
' ment should be prepared to make up any sums
' that may be wanting to afford adequate stipends
' to the family.'

Every obstacle was thrown in the way of the
realization of the property. The treasure was concealed under ground in the palace. A large amount
in gold mohurs was kept in the private apartments
of the Ranees, where it could not be taken.
Then the Ranees refused to point out what portion of the furniture and jewels they wished to
retain, and at other times they offered to give up

the whole, without retaining any part for themselves; and, on one occasion, the opposition culminated in a riot in the palace, in which several persons were injured.[1]

The Commissioner, Captain Elliot, appears to have acted with the greatest forbearance under these trying circumstances, and Lord Dalhousie directed,[2] that 'he should be exhorted to continue ' to act on the same principles, disregarding the ' petulance and vexatious opposition the Ranees ' may offer; and under every provocation showing ' them the courtesy due to their rank, their sex, ' and their changed condition; especially he should ' be instructed to have recourse to no "stringent or ' " coercive measures," without previous communi- ' cation with the Government, except under cir- ' cumstances which will not admit of delay.' And, again, when the retention of the gold mohurs was reported to him, he wrote to the Commissioner[3] :—' It will be satisfactory to the Govern- ' ment if the treasure withheld improperly in the

---

[1] Parl. Papers, Annexation of Berar, pp. 25, 32, 42.

[2] Lord Dalhousie's Minute, 30th September, 1854. Parl. Papers, Annexation of Berar, 1856, p. 29.

[3] Parl. Papers, Annexation of Berar, 1856, p. 45.

' palace, should be obtained by persuasion, or volun-
' tarily given up. Under any circumstances, you
' should closely adhere to the resolution expressed
' in your 12th paragraph, that you would on no
' account use force for the recovery of the gold
' mohurs. It would, indeed, be desirable rather
' to fail in obtaining them, than to enter the palace
' apartment for that purpose.'

Eventually the Ranees gave up some of the
gold mohurs, and some of the treasure was dug
up : but it was the opinion of the Commissioner
that large sums were still concealed, or had been
made away with. The difficulty as to the furniture
and jewels to be assigned to the Ranees, was solved
by the Commissioner making that selection for
them, which they refused to make for themselves.[1]

The property, after setting aside suitable portions of it for the Ranees, and after payment
of the debts of the household,[2] realized the sum

---

[1] Parliamentary Papers, Annexation of Berar, pp. 42, 43, 27.

[2] These debts should have been paid by the Rajah in his lifetime, and his money was ' now applied to the purpose on which it
' ought originally to have been expended.' See Lord Dalhousie's
Minute of the 26th of September, 1854. Parliamentary Papers,
Annexation of Berar, p. 30.

of 200,000*l.*[1] On the 26th of September, 1854, long before this sum was realized, Lord Dalhousie observed :—' The officiating Commissioner asks for ' the promised instructions regarding the formation ' of the fund for the use of the Ranees, to be ' formed out of the value of property to be sold ' for their behoof. The Government will not be ' in a condition to give those instructions until it ' shall know the sum which may have been realized, ' and shall have determined how it may be invested. ' In the meantime, the officiating Commissioner ' should pay the full amount of the several stipends ' allowed to the persons for whom they were ' designed, out of the Government Treasury.' Mr. Temple, the Commissioner of Nagpore, in his recent Report on that province, speaks of the above-mentioned sum of 200,000*l.* as constituting ' the ' Bhonsla Fund,' and as a deposit in the hands of the British Government for the benefit and support of the Bhonsla family. Notwithstanding this official declaration, to which Major Bell refers in his work, — notwithstanding the re-

---

[1] See Mr. TEMPLE's *Report* on Nagpore, and Parl. Papers, Annexation of Berar, p. 30.

peated declarations of Lord Dalhousie on this subject,—Major Bell has thought fit to write as follows:[1]—'In his very natural desire to overlay 'this ugly deed with a little moral gilding, Lord 'Dalhousie betrayed himself into some inconsistency 'of language, but his practical object is not at all 'ambiguous. He intended absolutely to appro-'priate the private property of the family, and 'with the proceeds to supply, or reduce as much as 'possible, the annual expense of their maintenance. 'He does indeed repeatedly declare that the pro-'ceeds shall not be "alienated from the Bhonsla '"family." But as he simultaneously employs in 'these very minutes, and in the orders issued at 'the same time to the Commissioner, other terms 'implying a totally opposite meaning, these pretty 'expressions become mere prevarications, and fail 'entirely to give an air of decency to what was, 'in fact, a daring act of spoliation.' I can find nothing in Lord Dalhousie's Minutes to justify these remarks. He may not have been sufficiently explicit as to the destination of this fund eventually, but he states expressly, that the fund was to be an inalienable deposit for the benefit of the Bhonsla

---

[1] BELL's *Empire in India*, p. 240.

family—a statement which would seem to exclude the Government from any participation in that fund. So long as it was so kept in deposit, all the annuities and pensions to the late Rajah's family, relations, and dependants—amounting to a sum far exceeding any interest the fund could produce,—were paid by the British Government. And although Lord Dalhousie did not explain how the fund was to be dealt with when the pensions were paid off, yet it is clear he set it apart, and appropriated it, as an inalienable fund for the benefit of the Bhonsla family, and that he left the fund untouched when he resigned office in 1856. Without pledging the Government of India as to details, Lord Dalhousie laid down a principle for the administration of the fund, and left it open to some future Governor-General to deal with it in accordance with such principle, that is, for the benefit of the Bhonsla family, in such manner as he might think just.[1]

---

[1] While this sheet has been in the press, the Calcutta Correspondent of the *Times* announces, that Sir C. Trevelyan has ' absorbed ' this fund, and ' capitalized ' it. I suppose this means that the money has been taken by the Government, and Government Paper substituted for it. But whatever is now done with

At the time of the annexation, Lord Dalhousie granted the following annuities to the ladies of the family of the late Rajah :—

The Banka Baee, adoptive mother
  of the late Rajah ....£12,000 a year.
The widows of the late Rajah :—

Unpoornah	£5,000	,,
Durga	2,500	,,
Annunda	2,500	,,
Kamulgee	2,500	,,
Sacotra	1,000	,,

£25,500 a year.

In addition to these stipends, the family held estates, free from payment of revenue, producing 5,000*l.* a year.

Lord Dalhousie likewise directed, that liberal provision should be made for other members of the family, as well as the connections, dependants, and retainers of the late Rajah. The total sum granted to these persons amounted to 78,700*l.* a year. Mr. Temple, in his recent Report, states, that notwithstanding the death of some of these annuitants, the sum of 98,200*l.*, one-fourth of the revenue of

the fund, I would only call attention to the fact, that the fund, which Lord Dalhousie is supposed to have appropriated, is actually in existence, and the subject of a financial operation, in 1865.

the late kingdom of Nagpore, was still devoted to the support of the Bhonsla family, and its retainers and dependants.

I trust this short statement will relieve Lord Dalhousie from the charge of spoliation. The creation of the Bhonsla Fund with the proceeds of the sale, and its present existence as an actual fund in the hands of the British Government, show that Lord Dalhousie's object was not confiscation, but preservation. If the property was sold at a great sacrifice, as Mr. Kaye suggests, that was a misfortune for which Lord Dalhousie is not shown to be answerable. It could not have been his wish to diminish a fund which, to some extent—so long as the Government held it in deposit without paying interest—diminished the amount payable by Government for annuities and pensions.

THE NAWAB OF THE CARNATIC.

On the 17th of October, 1855, his Highness Mahomed Ghouse, the last Nawab of the Carnatic,
died, without leaving issue. The Prince Azeem
Jah, his uncle and nearest relation, sought the
recognition of the Government as Nawab, in
succession to his nephew. The Government of
Madras, Lord Dalhousie, and the Court of Directors, all concurred in refusing to recognize his
claim.

The Nawabs of the Carnatic, once important
powers, with whom the kings of England cor-
responded, and the East India Company negotiated,
had long since dwindled into mere puppets of
royalty. In 1801, in consequence of their mis-
conduct during the war with Tippoo Sultan in

1799, and the subsequent discovery of a secret correspondence between them and that prince, they were deprived of the government of their country, and reduced to the position of sovereigns in name and rank only, with a handsome pecuniary pension secured on the revenues. Their position was somewhat similar to that of the late titular sovereign of Delhi; but to compare the condition to which they afterwards sank with that of fallen royalty elsewhere, would give a very inadequate notion of their degradation. The kings of Delhi, though shorn of real power, continued to reside in the imperial city, with the empty honours of a throne; they rarely came in contact with any functionary higher than a Commissioner, and on the rare occasions when they encountered a Governor-General, they were treated with extraordinary honours; and they retained, as the representatives of the house of Timour, their hold on the affections of the Mahommedans throughout India; and even Europeans could not refuse to feel for them something of that respect and sympathy which fallen greatness inspires. Very different was the position of the Nawabs of the Carnatic. Living in a presidency town, overshadowed by the Governor of Madras, squandering their large revenue in debauchery and mere frivolities; cheating, whenever they could cheat, their creditors by means of their immunity from legal process; and, on the other hand, plundered by usurers, whose rapacity was in proportion to the insecurity of their debts; they rapidly sank to the lowest limit to which puppet-royalty can descend. Such a mockery of an ancient dynasty could answer no useful purpose, though it might form a rallying point for the disaffected, and it can hardly be contended that the Government of India was bound to perpetuate so mischievous a " sham," at the expense of one-fifth of the revenues of the province, if it could be got rid of without injustice.

Two questions arose for consideration. First, whether Prince Azeem Jah had any hereditary right to succeed his nephew. Second, if he had not, whether it was under the circumstances expedient to confer the title of Nawab upon him.

No better statement of the argument on the hereditary right can be put, than that by Lord Dalhousie, in his Minute of the 19th of December, 1855 :—[1]

---

[1] Carnatic Papers, printed by order of the House of Commons, 17th April, 1860, p. 47, paragraphs 2, 3, 4, 5, and 6.

' In the determination of the future disposal of
' the musnud of the Carnatic, it is quite unnecessary
' to make any reference to the treaties of 1785,
' 1787, and 1792.

' Subsequently to the date of those treaties, it
' was declared by the British Government, that
' the detected treachery and secret but active hos-
' tility of the Nawabs Mahomed Ali and Omdut-ul-
' Omrah had placed them in the position of public
' enemies, had rendered their territories justly liable
' to forfeiture, and had therefore abrogated the
' treaties which had previously been in force.
' "By acting on these principles of conduct,"
' says Lord Wellesley, " the Nabobs have n
' " only violated the rights of the Company, but y
' " uniting their interests with those of the m st
' " implacable enemy of the British empire, act ly
' " placed themselves in the relation of   ic
' " enemies to the Company's government,   d
' again, " at the death of Omdut ul Omra   he
' " British Government remained at liberty to

---

¹ See paragraph 14 of the Marquis Wellesley's Despatch,
May, 1801, in 2nd vol. of Lord WELLESLEY'S *Indian Des*,
p. 520. The whole of this important despatch is not insert
Parliamentary papers,—only so much as appears in the Pe
Case. See also paragraphs 16 and 19 of this despatch.

' " exercise its rights, founded on the faithless
' " policy of its ally, in whatever manner might be
' " deemed most conducive to the immediate safety
' " and to the general interests of the Company in
' " the Carnatic."

' Thus in 1801, the territories of the Nawab of
' the Carnatic were at the absolute disposal of the
' British Government.[1]

' It is distinctly stated in Lord Wellesley's
' despatches, and in the papers connected with the
' treaty of 1801, that the British Government was
' then at liberty to assume the government of the
Carnatic. Lord Wellesley was only deterred from
assuming it by various considerations of expe-
diency and policy, in which the revolt of the
Poligars, the view which might be taken of the
measure by other native powers, or the long-
established connection between the Company and
the House of Mahomed Ali, all held a place.

Accordingly, the title of the Nawab of the
Carnatic was conferred upon Azeem-ul-Dowlah by
the treaty of 1801, on certain conditions which
are specified.

---

[1] See Lord Wellesley's despatch of 18th August, 1801.
Carnatic Parliamentary papers of the 27th May, 1861, p. 109.

'It is from this treaty, if at all, that a right of
'hereditary succession to the musnud of the Car-
'natic must be derived.'

Prince Azeem Jah and his advisers deny that
there was treachery or hostility on the part of the old
Nawabs, and they cite Mr. Mill's criticism on the
evidence of it.[1] Whether that criticism is satisfactory I need not stop to inquire, though I do not
think it would be difficult to show, that Lord Wellesley was justified in his conviction of the Nawab's
treachery. It is sufficient for my purpose to say,
that this question was considered in 1801, and had
long been *res judicata*. No statesman, in the po

---

[1] MILL's *History of British India*, vol. vi. p. 309. This cri
cism omits all mention of the fact that during the war aga
Tippoo, in 1799, the Nawab ' acted more like an enemy th
' friend,' and was suspected of treachery at the time by Lord
then Governor of Madras. The Nawab was prohibited by t
correspondence with foreign powers, and ought to have a
correspondence with such an enemy to our rule as Tippoo.
Malcolm, who was much better acquainted with Oriental
expression than Mr. Mill, considered the letters found at S
patam, contained ' conclusive evidence of a secret int
' between the Nawab and Tippoo Sultan, directed to p
' hostile to the interests of the Company.' See Narrative
ceedings relative to the settlement of the Carnatic b
(afterwards Sir John) Malcolm. Papers ordered by the
Commons to be printed, 17th April, 1860, pp. 23, 24, a

tion of Lords Dalhousie or Harris, could dream of re-opening in 1855, questions which had been settled in 1801. The question which they had to decide was, not whether Lord Wellesley was right in imposing the treaty of 1801 on the Nawab he then placed on the throne, but whether under the terms of that treaty, which had subsisted for upwards of half a century, they were justified in doing that which sound policy demanded, and in abating an admitted nuisance. The simple issue for their decision was, whether Lord Wellesley had undertaken, in the treaty of 1801, that the titular dignity and emoluments continued to the new Nawab should be hereditary.

The first Treaty signed by the new Nawab, Azeem-ul-Dowlah, was not ratified by Lord Wellesley as required by its concluding article. He objected to it, because the preamble and first section attributed the right of the new Nawab, Azeem-ul-Dowlah, to succeed ' to a supposed claim of inhe- ' ritance, and not to the liberality and moderation ' of the British Government.' ' This,' he observed, ' was the fundamental principle on which the late ' arrangements have been framed ; and consequently

'the acknowledgment of an inherent right in any
'member of the family of the late' Nawabs 'to
'succeed to the Soubahdarree of the Carnatic is
'incompatible with the maintenance of that prin-
'ciple.'[1]   In consequence of this objection, the
preamble and first article were altered.   The Treaty,
thus altered, received the cheerful assent[2] and signature of the Nawab Azeem-ul-Dowlah.   The important part of the preamble, and the whole of the
first article, thus altered, are as follows :[3]—

'And whereas, the Soubahdarry of Arcot having
'become vacant, the Prince Azeem-ul-Dowlah Ba-
'hadur has now been established by the English
'East India Company in the rank, property, and
'possessions *of his ancestors*, heretofore Nabobs of
'the Carnatic : And whereas the said Company
'and his Highness Prince Azeem-ul-Dowlah Ba-
'hadur have judged it expedient that additional
'provisions should be made for supplying the

---

[1] Despatch of the 18th of August, 1801.   Carnatic Parliamentary papers of May, 1861, p. 109.

[2] Despatch of the Governor of Madras to Vice-President in
Council, 22nd September, 1801, paragraphs 5 and 6.   Carnatic
papers of May, 1861, pp. 111 and 112.

[3] Vol. ii. Lord WELLESLEY's *Indian Despatches*, Appendix,
p. 720.

' defects of all former engagements, and of esta-
' blishing the connection between the said con-
' tracting parties on a permanent basis of security
' *in all times to come :* Wherefore, the following
' treaty is now established,' &c. . . . . . *for settling*
the succession to the Soubahdarry of the territories
of Arcot, and for vesting the administration of the
civil and military government of the Carnatic in
the United Company, &c.

' Article 1. The Nabob Azeem-ul-Dowlah Ba-
' hadur is hereby formally established in the state
' and rank, with the dignities dependent thereon of
' his ancestors, heretofore Nabobs of the Carnatic,
' and the possession thereof is hereby guaranteed
' by the Honourable East India Company to his
' said Highness Azeem-ul-Dowlah Bahadur, who
' has accordingly succeeded to the Soubahdarry of
' the territories of Arcot.'

By the fourth article, the whole civil, military,
fiscal, and judicial government of the Carnatic was
vested for ever in the East India Company.

Speaking of this Treaty, Lord Dalhousie observes :—' I entirely agree with Lord Harris, and
' with the members of the Government of Fort

' St. George, in holding that the treaty of 1801
' confers no right of hereditary succession. It is
' a purely .personal treaty concluded between the
' Honourable Company on the one part, and the
' Nawab Azeem-ul-Dowlah on his own behalf on
' the other part. There is no mention of heirs and
' successors in any part of the treaty, and no grant
' of anything is made by it to any one except to the
' Nawab Azeem-ul-Dowlah himself. Lord Wellesley
' was not a man who did things without a reason.
' When, therefore, Lord Wellesley, while nego-
' tiating treaties with the Nawab of Oude and
' others, and forming the treaties with these
' princes, their heirs and successors, is found
' negotiating a treaty with the Nawab Azeem-ul-
' Dowlah alone, and omitting all mention in it
' of heirs and successors, it is very certain that
' Lord Wellesley did not intend to extend the
' provisions of that treaty beyond the life of
' Azeem-ul-Dowlah himself.'

The words, ' of his ancestors,' occurring in the
preamble and first article, are relied on as showing,
that Azeem-ul-Dowlah succeeded by descent from
his ancestors. But those words only state, what
was the fact, that the former Nawabs were the

ancestors of Azeem-ul-Dowlah, without in any way affirming that he inherited from them. The Treaty does not say that he succeeded, but that he was ' established ' in the rank of his ancestors. Lord Wellesley was careful to erase from the first Treaty the words, 'the right of Prince Azeem-' ul-Dowlah, founded upon the hereditary right of ' his. father, to succeed to the rank,' and to substitute instead the words, 'established in the rank,' and to declare, as we have seen, that Azeem-ul-Dowlah did not succeed by hereditary right, but in consequence of the liberality and moderation of the British Government. As a matter of fact, Azeem-ul-Dowlah was not the heir of the late Nawab in 1801, for Ali Hossein, the son of the late Nawab, was at that time such heir.[1] Azeem- ul-Dowlah moreover relinquished all claim to the acknowledgment of his hereditary pretensions,[2]

---

[1] In some of the despatches Ali Hossein is spoken of as the reputed son of the late Nawab. He was the acknowledged son of the late Nawab, who made a will in his favour ; and the acknowledgment of a son by his father is almost conclusive as to parentage, according to Mahomedan law.—MACNAGHTEN'S *Principles of Mahomedan Law*, p. 61.

[2] See paragraph 6 of the letter of the Governor of Madras to the President in Council, dated 22nd September, 1801, in Carnatic Parliamentary papers of May, 1861, p. 112.

and took possession of the throne under a new title, which was not derived from the old Nawabs, but from the treaty of 1801.

Mr. Arnold contends that the Treaty was not a personal one, because he says, ' the fourth article ' declares that four-fifths of the revenue were *for* ' *ever* vested in the Company, and the remaining ' one-fifth *for ever* appropriated for the support of ' the dignity of the Nawabship.'[1] But this does not accurately represent the fact, for the fourth article contains no such words. It provides that the administration of the civil and military government of the Carnatic, ' together with the full and ' exclusive right to the revenues thereof, (with the ' exception of such portion of such revenues as shall ' be appropriated for the maintenance of the said ' Nabob, and for the support of *his* dignity,) shall be ' for ever vested in the said English Company.'[2] This article not only does not secure one-fifth of the revenues to the Nabob *for ever*, but limits the

---

[1] ARNOLD's *Dalhousie Administration*, vol. ii. pp. 176, 177.

[2] See Lord WELLESLEY's *Indian Despatches*, vol. ii. Appendix, p. 721. The 6th article also speaks of the fifth of the revenues being ' allotted for the maintenance of the said Nawab and the ' support of his dignity.'

payment of revenue to the 'said Nabob,' that is,
to Azeem-ul-Dowlah. All the revenue is vested in
the Company, except what is excepted, and the
exception does not confer more than a life-interest
on Azeem-ul-Dowlah.

Great stress is also laid on the words, 'in all
times to come,' found in the preamble of the
Treaty, and in the second Separate Article.[1] It
is said, these words show that the treaty was not
a personal one, that it contemplated the existence
of Nawabs in all times to come, and therefore an
hereditary succession. If the intention had been to
create an hereditary title, nothing would have been
easier than to say so in express words, and it might
have been inconvenient and impolitic, even having
regard to the interests of the Nawab, to limit the
tenure in express terms to his life. The framers of
the Treaty might well content themselves with the
words used in the first article, which established
Azeem-ul-Dowlah alone on the throne, and guaranteed it to him alone, and omitted the usual
limitation in favour of heirs and successors, found in

---

[1] Vol. ii. of Lord WELLESLEY's *Indian Despatches*, Appendix,
pp. 720, 723.

other treaties establishing sovereignties.[1] Are these
considerations outweighed by the fact that the
words 'in all times to come' are found in the
preamble? Surely, if it had been the intention
of the parties to create an hereditary title by
these words, we should not have found them in
the preamble alone, but also in the first article,
which defines the rights of the Nawab.   The
explanation of these words which I would suggest,
is that the framers of this Treaty intended it to
operate in perpetuity so far as it was expressed,
that is, so far as the rights of the Company were
concerned, leaving it to be determined, by future
considerations and events, whether this shadowy
royalty should be prolonged beyond the life of
Azeem-ul-Dowlah. The Treaty, therefore, carefully
confines the tenure of the Nawabship to the life of
Azeem-ul-Dowlah, and yet speaks in a vague way
so as not to exclude the possibility of the existence
of future Nawabs. This possibility might well be
contemplated, and yet confer no hereditary right of
succession, and it is clear that a mere reference to

---

[1] See the treaties of Sattarah, Jhansi, and Nagpore already
referred to.

future Nawabs, does not make them parties to a
Treaty which conferred no benefit on them, and was
entered into by Azeem-ul-Dowlah ' on his own
' behalf' alone.[1]

Mr. Arnold also cites the second Separate Article,
to show that the Treaty was not a personal one.[2]
That article states, that it is ' the intention of the
' contracting parties that the said sum of 213,421
' pagodas, and the said sum of 621,105 pagodas,
' shall be considered to be *permanent* deductions *in*
' *all times to come* from the revenues of the Car-
' natic.'[3]   Now this sum of 213,421 pagodas was a
sum payable, under the ninth article of the treaty
of 1787, to the family and principal officers of two
former .Nabobs, and the sum of 621,105 pagodas
was payable on account of the private debts of one
of those Nabobs, and the sixth article of the Treaty
of 1801 provided, that both these sums should be
deducted from the gross revenue, in order to ascertain the net revenue, of which the Nawab was to
have one-fifth.   It is obvious, that as these debts

---

[1] See Preamble of Treaty of 1801.

[2] ARNOLD's *Dalhousie Administration*, vol. ii., p 177.

[3] Lord WELLESLEY's *Indian Despatches*, vol. ii. Appendix,
p. 723.

were paid off, and as the relatives and officers of these old Nawabs died, these large sums would decrease in amount, and the net revenue would increase. To prevent this, and to secure to the Government these large deductions from the revenue, even after the debts and pensions were paid, this clause was imposed on the Nabob. The word ' permanent' is not used in the sense of 'perpetual,' but with the view of showing that the charges were to continue, though the objects for which they were incurred should fail. The words 'in all times to come' have already been commented on. They cannot be regarded as words of hereditary limitation. It would be more consonant with established rules of construction to reject those words altogether, than give them a scope and operation inconsistent with their position in the Treaty, and the other language of that document.

Another argument on the Treaty is founded on the words found in the preamble, 'for settling the ' succession to the Soubahdarry.' The suggestion seems to be, that these words contemplate an hereditary succession. But Lord Harris has well observed in his Minute, that these words refer to the vacant throne mentioned in the former part of the

7

preamble,[1] and were fully satisfied by the appointment of Azeem-ul-Dowlah to that throne.

Lord Dalhousie's Minute thus continues,—It
' is true that two Nawabs have sat upon the
' musnud since the death of Azeem-ul-Dowlah, but
' they successfully occupied that position solely by
' the grace and favour of the British Government,
' and not as of right. There is nothing whatever
' connected with the accession of those princes to
' the musnud, which would countenance the asser-
' tion of any right to that dignity, either in them-
' selves or in their children or heirs.'

' The uncle of the late Nawab supports his
' present claim to the succession by reference to
' certain allusions which have been made to him
' in former official papers, as the heir of his nephew
' Mahomet Ghouse. Undoubtedly, those allusions
' were made ; no attempt need be made to evade
' them or weaken the full force of their meaning,
' such as it is. They may readily be admitted to
' indicate an expectation on the part of the British
' Government, that if Mahomet Ghouse should

---

[1] Minute of Lord Harris, dated 25th October, 1855, para. 19.
Carnatic papers of April 17, 1860, p. 10.

'have no children, his uncle Azeem Jah would
'be allowed to succeed him as Nawab.   But to
'indicate an expectation, or even an intention,
'is not to recognize or confer a right.   The words,
'therefore, which have been quoted, conferred no
'right on Azeem Jah, and conveyed no pledge or
'promise of the succession to him ; and, although
'they indicated a favourable intention on the part
'of the Government towards him, the Government
'has since had but too much reason to forego all
'such intentions in favour of himself and the
'members of his family.'

I should exceed the limits to which this work is
confined, if I supported these statements of Lord
Dalhousie with a narrative of the correspondence
which took place on the subsequent accessions of
the son and grandson of Azeem-ul-Dowlah.[1]   I
would only remark, that on the death of Azeem-
ul-Dowlah in 1819, the Madras Government,
finding no hereditary limitation in the Treaty,
felt precluded from acknowledging his eldest son

---

[1] For a statement of the correspondence, see Carnatic Parliamentary papers of 17th April, 1860, pp. 34, 35, and paragraph 6 of the Despatch of the Court of Directors, 15th March,
1856, at p. 45 of those papers.

as his successor, and applied to the Governor-General for instructions, and when the rank and title of Nawab was conceded to the son, his gratitude was expressed in language implying the reception of a great favour, rather than the recognition of his rights.[1]

The alleged admissions of the Government, and the circumstances attending them, were not thought worthy of explanation by Lord Dalhousie, but the facts are as follows :—

In 1829, on the occasion of the appointment of Mr. Scott as physician to the Nawab, the Court of Directors wrote :—' We disapprove of the prin- ' ciple of this arrangement, but under the peculiar ' circumstances of the case, the Nawab being an ' infant and in delicate health, and the Naib-i- ' Moktar.(Azeem Jah) being the next heir, in case ' of his demise, the appointment of Mr. Scott ' admits of justification.'[2]

And in 1843, when the list of natives claiming exemption from the jurisdiction of the Supreme Court was revised, the Marquis of Tweedale in

---

[1] See his letter of the 17th September, 1819. Carnatic Parliamentary papers, printed 17th April, 1860, pp. 16, 35.

[2] Carnatic papers, printed 17th April, 1860, p. 15.

Council observed,—' That his Highness the Prince
' Azeem Jah Bahadur (the late Naib-i-Moktar) does
' not hold that place in list No. 1, to which he is
' entitled, in consideration of the position he has
' lately occupied in communication with the British
' Government, and of that which he still holds in
' relation to his Highness the Nawab, and to his
' succession to the musnud. It is, therefore, re-
' solved, that the name of Prince Azeem Jah be
' placed first on the list of such relations of his
' Highness,'[1] &c.

Now we have the best authority for saying
that, as a matter of fact, the first of these alleged
admissions did not refer to the inheritance of
the Nawabs. The Court of Directors, in their
despatch of the 15th of March, 1856, observe :[2]—
' The subject then before us was not the suc-
' cession to the musnud, but the appointment of
' a physician to the young Nawab, and we had no
' intention whatever of entering into the question,
' what might be Azeem Jah's right of inheritance.
' As the nearest of kin, we spoke of him as the
' heir to whatever could legally be derived from

---

[1] Carnatic Parliamentary papers, printed 17th April, 1860, p. 9.
[2] *Ibid.*, para. 8, p. 46.

' the Nawab by inheritance, but the Nawabship
' had never been considered by us to be heritable
' by heirs as of right.'

Admissions to be of value must be made with
reference to the subject, and should not be inci-
dental observations, made in the discussion of such
unimportant questions as whether a doctor should
be appointed, or a name stood in its proper place
in a list.   The succession to the throne was not in
question on either of these occasions, but if it had
been, these observations would not have had the
effect of importing new terms into the Treaty.   The
Treaty either conferred an hereditary title on Azeem
Jah, or it did not.   If it did, the alleged admissions
are not wanted,—if it did not, the alleged admissions did not by their own force create an hereditary
title, and could not be imported into the Treaty so
as to alter its language into an hereditary grant.

On the question of policy, I shall rest entirely
on the very clear view of it held by Lord Harris.
Mr. Arnold erroneously ascribes the following
passage to Lord Dalhousie,[1] but the Governor-

---

[1] ARNOLD's *Dalhousie Administration*, vol. ii., p. 175.

General felt that he could add nothing to the force of Lord Harris's observations on this head, and contented himself with a reference to his lordship's Minute.[1]   Lord Harris observes,[2]—

'I will here state my very decided opinion that 'these rights and privileges should not be continued, 'if they can be abrogated without a violation of 'faith.

'First, on the general principle that the 'semblance of royalty, without any of the power, is 'a mockery of authority which must be pernicious.

'Second, because though there is virtually no 'divided rule or co-ordinate authority in the govern- 'ment of the country—for these points were finally 'settled by the Treaty of 1801—yet some appear- 'ance of so baneful a system is still kept up by the 'continuance of a quasi royal family and court.

'Third, because the legislation of the country 'being solely in the hands of the Honourable Court, 'it is not only anomalous, but prejudicial to the 'community, that a separate authority, not amenable 'to the law, should be permitted to exist.

---

[1] See LORD DALHOUSIE's *Minute* of 19th December, 1855. Parliamentary Carnatic papers of April, 1860, p. 48.

[2] Carnatic papers of April, 1860, paragraph 6, p. 9.

'Fourth, because it is impolitic and unwise to
'allow a pageant to continue, which though it has
'been politically harmless, may at any time become
'a nucleus for sedition and agitation.

'Fifth, because the habits of life and course of
'proceeding of the Nabobs have been morally most
'pernicious, tending to bring high station into
'disrepute, and favouring the accumulation of an
'idle and dissipated population in the chief city of
'the Presidency. . . . .

'50.[1] I think there are strong reasons for alter-
'ing the relations of this government with the Arcot
'family, and of changing its position.

'The causes which may have given force to the
'policy of 1801 no longer exist; the rank, con-
'sequence, and reputation of the Arcot family have
'sunk by the conduct of its representatives. The
'manner of life and the character of the late Nabob
'were disreputable, and the conduct of the Prince
'Azeem Jah, who would succeed him, has already
'come under the severe animadversion of the
'Honourable Court.

'It is with no wish unnecessarily to bring these

---

[1] Carnatic papers, printed 17th April, 1860, p. 13.

'faults into public view that I make mention of
'them, but because I am convinced that serious
'moral evil is caused by the continuance of the
'pageant of an effete royalty, and that political
'inconvenience might at any time arise from the
'existence of a Court at the Presidency, which,
'though destitute of authority and power, must be
'inimical, or at all events discontented, and capable
'of being made a nucleus for intrigue.'

These words require no comment from me.
The conduct of the titular Sovereign of Delhi in
1857, and the gathering of the disaffected around
that shadow of the Great Mogul, have sufficiently
illustrated the wisdom of these remarks.

The members of the late Nawab's family were
liberally provided for,[1] as well as his officers and
attendants. The Government also undertook to
pay all his debts, and these, as well as others
contracted by Prince Azeem Jah, when acting as
Naib during his nephew's minority, amounting in
the whole to the large sum of 420,000*l.*,[2] have been
paid by the Government.

---

[1] Prince Azeem Jah was allowed 15,000*l.* a year.

[2] See speech of Sir C. Wood in the last Carnatic Debate,
Times, 15th March, 1865.

THE RAJ OF TANJORE.

THE Rajahs of Tanjore were formerly independent princes, but in the year 1799, a Treaty was concluded with the Rajah Serfojee, whereby the whole country of Tanjore, except its fort, was transferred to the British Government. The Rajah remained the titular sovereign of Tanjore, and the actual sovereign of the fort, in which he resided.

On the 29th of October, 1855, Sewajee, the last Rajah of Tanjore, died, leaving two daughters, and no less than twenty widows.

Mr. Forbes, then Resident at Tanjore, with the consent of the family, proposed that the youngest daughter should be elevated to the throne, as the eldest daughter was in a dying state. He cited well-known authorities, showing that in the case of private individuals, females inherit in default of male issue, and he mentioned the fact, that in the year 1735, the widow of a deceased Rajah of Tanjore had succeeded to the throne.

Lord Dalhousie was on his way from the Nilgherries to Calcutta, and was present at the Council in Madras when the subject came before it. It was then unanimously resolved, that the Raj was extinct.[1] The case came before Lord Dalhousie again when presiding at the Supreme Council in Calcutta, and he came to the same conclusion, which was supported by all the members of his Council.[2]

The case presented three questions for consideration. First, whether there was any male heir of the last Rajah. Second, whether, in the absence of a male heir, the daughter could inherit. And third, whether, if there were no inheritance, it was expedient to reconstitute the Raj, and give it to the daughter.

First, there was no male heir of the late Rajah. He left neither a real nor an adopted son, and he

---

[1] The members of the Madras Government were :—Lord Harris, Governor ; General Anson, Commander-in-chief ; and Sir H. Montgomery.

[2] The members of the Supreme Council were Mr. Dorin, Sir J. P. Grant, and Sir B. Peacock.

was himself the only son of his father, the Rajah
Serfojee, who was the adopted son of his predecessor,
Tooljajee, consequently any claimant through males
must have been distantly related. No such claimant
appeared.

On the second question, Mr. Arnold observes,—
' This was a house in which, contrary to Hindoo
' custom, no salic law ruled—the widow or daughter
' might succeed the husband or father.'[1]   There is
no other foundation for this statement, than the
fact that a widow succeeded to the Raj in 1735, but
the circumstances attending that succession are not
stated. If this succession proved anything, it would
establish the right of the senior widow to the Raj,
but it would be too much to infer from this single
circumstance, the existence of a right in the widow
in this particular family, unknown to the general
custom of descent. Still less could it be inferred
from this succession that a right also accrued to the
daughter, who alone claimed it from Lord Dalhousie.
No law or authority has been cited, showing that
females can inherit a Raj, and all the members of
Council at Calcutta and Madras, men conversant

---

[1] ARNOLD'S *Dalhousie Administration*, vol. ii., p. 182.

with such questions, agreed with Lords Dalhousie and Harris in their opinion, that the daughter could not inherit. The Court of Directors held, that ' by ' no law or usage has the daughter of a Hindoo ' Rajah any right of succession to a Raj ;'[1] and Sir C. Trevelyan, when he, as Governor of Madras, reviewed all the circumstances of the case, observed,[2] —' My first twelve years of public service were passed ' in the Indian diplomatic departments, and I have ' as extensive a knowledge of the customs and ' practice of native chiefs as most people. I men- ' tion this as my justification for offering a con- ' fident opinion, that the succession of females forms ' no part of the constitution of native states or ' chiefships. It may occasionally have taken place, ' as in the instance of Holkar's widow, Aralaya ' Bhai, and the Begum Sumroo, but the special ' nature of the circumstances in these cases, shows ' that it was a deviation from an established rule. ' No well-informed and impartial native would main- ' tain the right of succession of a female to a ' Hindoo Raj.'

---

[1] See the despatch of Court of Directors dated 16th April, 1856.
[2] See MOORE's *Indian Appeal Cases*, vol. vii., p. 542.

As females could not inherit, it was thought
that the Raj lapsed for want of heirs, and the only
question which remained for consideration was,
whether it was expedient to reconstitute the Raj,
and give it to the daughter. This question was
thus disposed of by Lord Dalhousie. 'When we
' know that more than fifty years ago the adminis-
' tration of Tanjore was formally withdrawn from
' the hands of its ruler, by reason of past misgovern-
' ment—when we learn from the Resident that
' even the late Rajah, shorn as he was of all power,
' yet betrayed a disposition on all occasions, "to
' " do whatever he knew the Resident would not
' " allow, and to use the whole weight of his authority
' " to frustrate whatever management might be
' " proposed for the advantage of the durbar ;" and
' when we are informed, "that the Rajah so far
' " succeeded, that it will certainly take time, and
' " thought, and care, to set straight all that the
' " late Rajah has put in disorder," I certainly think
' the British Government would be deeply to blame
' if it revived this dead sovereign in the person of
' a young girl, who, helpless now, would be nothing
' less than a tool in the mischievious hands of
' others in future years.' And the Court of Directors,

after observing that the daughter had no right to
succeed to the Raj, remarked [1]—' that it was entirely
' out of the question that we should create such
' a right, for the sole purpose of perpetuating a
' titular principality, at a great cost to the public
' revenues.'

Even those who consider the existence of native
states so desirable, that they would go out of their
way to recreate them when extinct, would find it
difficult to assign reasons for reconstituting the Raj
of Tanjore. It was not a native State. The Rajah
was a titular Prince, with neither subjects nor
territory beyond the walls of his fort. He had no
power to do good either to Tanjore, or the British
Government. His Raj was a sham royalty, involving a great charge on our revenues, and like other
sham royalties, it had been an annoyance to us, and
might probably become still more so in troubled
times.

As my own opinion in this case differs from the
view taken of it by so many eminent men, I must
be understood as expressing it with some diffidence.
I am inclined to think that this was not a case of

[1] Despatch of Court of Directors, 16th of April, 1856.

lapse or escheat; that the titular dignity expired; and that the sovereignty of the fort became
vacant.   Neither the daughter nor widow could
inherit.   On the other hand, as the Rajah was not
a dependent sovereign created by the British, but
held his fort as a reserved portion of his old
dominions, it was not a fief, which could lapse or
escheat to the British Government.   If I am
correct in this view, then it was the case of
the sovereign of the surrounding country taking
possession of the vacant sovereignty of the fort, no
other person having an equal claim to it.[1]   The
British Government could neither allow the sovereignty to remain vacant, nor permit any one else,
without title, to assume such sovereignty.

Mr. Arnold observes on this subject,[2]—' True to
' the steady policy of seizing every chance of
' aggrandisement, Lord Dalhousie refused to recog-
' nize any one of them ' (the widow and daughters)
' as successor, equally as it must appear against
' treaty and precedent.   A rich set of Jaghires, the
' estate of the mother of Sewajee, yielding three lacs

---

[1] I am speaking, of course, of the sovereign rights only, and
not of property.

[2] ARNOLD'S *Dalhousie Administration*, vol. ii., p. 182.

'of rupees annually, *was confiscated at the same time.*
'The Ranee of Tanjore appealed from Calcutta to
'Leadenhall Street, thence to the Supreme Court at
'Madras, and claimed 700,000*l.* as the property of
'her husband. Madras decided in her favour, but
'the Company appealed to the Privy Council. The
'Privy Council reversed the Indian decision, and
'only upon the ground that, as the Governor-
'General had acted for the Company in his interpre-
'tation of a treaty, a law court could take no
'cognizance of the Ranee's plaints. To the property
'and the titular dignity of Tanjore Lord Kingsdown
'declared that the Company had no *legal* claim,'
&c. In another passage,[1] Mr. Arnold states that
Lord Dalhousie, 'by a technicality of law courts,
'refused to the Ranee of Tanjore the crown and the
'treasure that belonged to her.'

In these passages there are some important
inaccuracies. No part of the Jaghires or lands
belonging to the Rajah or his family was taken
possession of, much less confiscated, during Lord
Dalhousie's administration. He left India in the
beginning of March, 1856, having done no more

---

[1] ARNOLD's *Dalhousie Administration*, vol. ii. p. 200.

than recommended that the Raj should be declared extinct.[1] The decision of the Court of Directors is dated the 16th of April, 1856, and after its arrival in India, Mr. Forbes, the former Resident, was appointed Commissioner at Tanjore, and, on the 18th of October, 1856, he assumed charge of all the lands belonging to the late Rajah and his family, with the view of investigating their titles, and ascertaining whether they were private or state property.[2] He also took possession of considerable personal property. Without awaiting the result of the investigation, the Ranee Kamachee, the senior widow, on the 16th of November, 1856, filed her bill in the Supreme Court at Madras, stating that the private and personal estate of the late Rajah had been taken possesion of by Mr. Forbes, and claiming such estate, but setting up no title to the Raj.[3] The Government in their answer insisted, that their

---

[1] By an order of the Government, even the pensions and allowances to the relations and dependants of the late Rajah were continued, pending the decision of the Court of Directors. See letter of Madras Government to Government of India, dated 10th July, 1856.

[2] See judgment of Lord Kingsdown. MOORE's *East Indian Appeals*, vol. vii. p. 538.

[3] MOORE's *East Indian Appeals*, vol. vii. p. 476.

right to take possession of the Rajah's estate, was a question of state, arising from the political relations between the East India Company and the state of Tanjore, and were matters which could not be inquired into by the Supreme Court. The answer, however, without waiving this objection, admitted that some of the real and personal property, specified in four different schedules, was private property of the late Rajah, which they were willing to deliver up to his legal representative.[1] The answer also stated, that the Government had resolved to appropriate the property mentioned in schedules M and N, for payment of the late Rajah's debts, and towards making a provision for his family.[2] The Supreme Court at Madras decided in the Ranee's favour, but the Privy Council were of opinion, that the property claimed by the respondent was seized by the British Government, acting as a sovereign power, and that the act so done, was an act of state, over which the Supreme Court had no jurisdiction. After this

---

[1] I suspect the answer admitted the same with respect to the property mentioned in another schedule, R, but the Report is not clear on this point. See Moore's *Indian Appeals*, vol. vii. p. 491.

[2] Moore's *East Indian Appeals*, vol. vii. p. 491.

decision, that portion of the property which was admitted to be private, and also, the whole of the landed estates,[1] were given up by the Government to the family of the late Rajah.

It thus appears that Lord Dalhousie had nothing to do with the seizure of this property; that the lands were never confiscated; that the personalty was not confiscated, but only such part of it was taken as appeared to appertain to the Raj; and that the assertion that Lord Dalhousie resorted to 'a ' technicality of the law courts' to deprive the Ranee of her crown and treasure, is perfectly unfounded, inasmuch as he had left India long before the suit was instituted, in which that defence was relied on.

---

[1] Chiefly through the exertions of my valued friend, the late Mr. Morehead, member of Council, and, for a short time, Governor of Madras.

ANNEXATION OF OUDE.

As Lord Dalhousie's advice with respect to Oude was not followed, and as he is not, in fact, responsible for the annexation of that province, it may seem a work of supererogation to examine his opinions on that subject. But as the annexation took place during his administration, as the general public still suppose that this was the final measure of his annexation policy, and as those better informed do not appreciate the advice he gave, I shall attempt to explain his views. To do this effectually, I must first consider, as briefly as possible, the nature of our relations with Oude.

By the 3rd article of the Treaty of 1801, the British Government bound itself ' to defend the

' territories of the Nawab Vizier of Oude against
' all foreign and domestic enemies,' and by the
6th article, the Nawab Vizier engaged that he
would ' establish in his reserved dominions, such
' a system of administration to be carried into
' effect by his own officers as shall be conducive
' to the prosperity of his subjects, and be calculated
' to secure the lives and property of the inhabitants,
' and his Excellency[1] will always advise with, and
' act in conformity to, the counsel of the officers of
' the East India Company.'

No system of government better calculated to
ensure failure was ever devised. The monarch was
rendered independent of his people. However
nefarious his conduct might be, he was protected
from their resentment. Nevertheless the government had all the elements of weakness, for it had no
strength of its own—for advice the King was bound
to listen to the minister of a foreign country—for
all purposes of coercion he was dependent on
British troops. All the evils of a divided government were secured for the country. The people

---

[1] That is, the Nawab Vizier. These Nawab Viziers subsequently, with the consent of our Government, assumed the title
of Kings of Oude.

soon discovered that there was another power beside the throne, stronger than the king himself. The favour of the Resident was a matter of the greatest moment, and a large class soon arose, protected from their own King, by the pledged faith of the British Government.[1]   Such a system led to its natural result, in the indifference of the Sovereign to good government, the destruction of his authority, and the contempt of his subjects. Lord Wellesley himself contemplated failure: ' I ' am satisfied,'[2] he said, ' that no effectual security ' can be provided against the ruin of the province ' of Oude until the exclusive management of the ' civil and military government of that country ' shall be transferred to the Company, under ' suitable provisions for the maintenance of his ' Excellency and family.'

That which was anticipated came to pass. The Kings of Oude, secured by British troops from the rebellion of their subjects, became indifferent or averse to the cares of government, gave themselves

---

[1] See Colonel Low's *Minute* of 18th August, 1855. Oude papers, p. 221.

[2] Lord WELLESLEY's *Despatches*, 22nd January, 1801, vol. ii. p. 426.

up to sensual indulgences, and confided the reins of power to the lowest creatures of their Court. The great landowners either bribed the Court functionaries and got their estates assessed at a trifling sum, or defied the collectors and refused payment of revenue, which was then collected by British bayonets. The lower orders were oppressed by the talookdars and farmers of the revenue. The police were few and untrust-worthy. The judges considered their cases, as barristers do their briefs, ' as things out of which ' money might be made.'[1] Corruption prevailed everywhere. Life and property were insecure, and violence and outrage were unchecked by police or courts of justice.

It was the duty of those who had inflicted this bad system on the people of Oude, to take some measures for their protection. But years passed away, and we did nothing but remonstrate occa-sionally with the King. In 1831, Lord William Bentinck went so far as to tell him, that ' unless ' his territories were governed upon other princi-

---

[1] Colonel SLEEMAN's *Report*, September 24, 1849, paragraph 16. Oude papers, p. 159.

' ples than those hitherto followed, and the
' prosperity of the people made the principal object
' of his administration, the precedents afforded by
' the principalities of the Carnatic and Tanjore
' would be applied to the kingdom of Oude, and
' to the entire management of the country, and the
' king would be transmuted into a state prisoner ' !
This threat also failed to have any effect, and the
state of the country remained the same during the
life of the King Nussurooddeen.   He was a con-
temptible creature, given up to the lowest
debauchery, but, if he had possessed the highest
intellectual powers, he would have found it difficult
to govern an Asiatic kingdom, under such a system
as that inaugurated by the Treaty of 1801.

His death took place in 1837, and Lord
Auckland thought this a favourable opportunity
for making a new treaty with his successor.
Lord Auckland considered this desirable, because
the Treaty of 1801 merely stipulated for a
power of control, without defining the means
of enforcing it, and this he proposed to remedy
by inserting in the new treaty a specific penalty,
to be incurred by the King, in case the misgovernment of the country should continue.

Few treaties do assign any penalty for the non-performance of their stipulations. If they are not observed, the party injured has a right to annul the treaty, or enforce its stipulations by a resort to arms. But Lord Auckland considered, as Lord Dalhousie likewise thought at a subsequent period, that it was impossible to enforce the stipulation of a treaty, which required reforms to be carried out by the king's own officers,—that the treaty imposed by the British Government on the Kings of Oude, having designated the King's own officers as the proper instruments for carrying out the proposed reforms, it would be unjust in the British Government to resort to force, because its own instruments did not succeed in carrying them out.

The Treaty of the 18th of September, 1837,[1] was accordingly signed by the King of Oude. After stipulating for the payment of an auxiliary force by the King, its 7th Article provided ' that ' the King of Oude will take into his immediate ' and earnest consideration, in concert with the ' British Resident, the best means of remedying

---

[1] See Oude papers, ordered to be printed 15th March, 1858, p. 33.

' the existing defects in the police, and in the
' judicial and revenue administration of his do-
' minions; and that if his Majesty should neglect
' to attend to the advice and counsel of the British
' Government or its local representative, and if
' (which God forbid) gross and systematic oppres-
' sion, anarchy, and misrule should hereafter at
' any time prevail within the Oude dominions,
' such as seriously to endanger the public tran-
' quillity, the British Government reserves to
' itself the right of appointing its own officers to
' the management of whatsoever portions of the
' Oude territory, either to a small or to a great
' extent, in which such misrule may have occurred,
' *for so long a period as it may deem necessary, the*
' *surplus receipts, in such a case, after defraying all*
' *charges, to be paid into the King's Treasury, and a*
' *true and faithful account rendered to his Majesty*
' *of the receipt and expenditure of the territories so*
' *assumed.'* The 8th Article provided, that ' if the
' Governor-General should exercise the power vested
' in him by the last Article, he would endeavour
' as far as possible to maintain (with such im-
' provements as they may admit of) the native
' institutions and forms of administration within

' the assumed territories, *so as to facilitate the restora-*
' *tion of these territories to the Sovereign of Oude,*
' *when the proper period for such restoration shall*
' *arrive.*'

The Court of Directors refused to ratify this
Treaty. By their despatch of the 15th of April, 1839,[1]
they directed that no delay should take place in
announcing to the King their disallowance of the
Treaty of 1837, and the restoration of their relations with the State of Oude to the footing on
which they previously stood. Instead of doing
this, however, the Governor-General adopted the
singular course of informing the King, that he was
released from the onerous condition, imposed on
him by the Treaty, of paying for the auxiliary force.
He did not mention the fact that the whole Treaty
was disallowed,[2] and, on the contrary, the intima-
tion of the disallowance of one part of it, was calculated to lead the King to believe, that in all other
respects it was in full force. Lord Auckland made

---

[1] Oude papers, ordered to be printed 15th March, 1858,
p. 57.

[2] See the letter of the Governor-General to the King of Oude,
dated 8th July, 1839. Oude papers, ordered to be printed
15th March, 1858, p. 60.

no secret of what he had thus done. In a letter to the Court of Directors, dated the 15th of July, 1839, he acknowledged the receipt of their orders of the 15th of April, and forwarded a copy of the letter he had addressed to the King of Oude.[1] The Court of Directors do not appear to have taken any notice of this strange mode of carrying out their orders.

It was not surprising that no progress was made in the improvement of the Government, for the Kings of Oude now felt perfectly safe. They thought the Treaty of 1837 was in existence, and that the worst that could befal them was a temporary relief from the trouble of governing, while all the royal honours and revenues would be preserved to them and their posterity. No language can describe the licentiousness of the Court, the corruption of the courtiers, the tyranny of the Talookdars, or the cruel wrongs of the people.

In December, 1847, Lord Hardinge had an interview with the King of Oude, and at the same time he addressed a memorandum[2] to him, in which

---

[1] See Oude papers, ordered to be printed 15th March, 1858, p. 60.

[2] Oude papers, ordered to be printed 15th March, 1858, p. 61.

he cited the Treaty of 1837 as if it were still in force,[1] and warned the King, that if he procrastinated in making the necessary reforms, he would incur the risk of forcing the British authorities to interfere

---

[1] The following are extracts from this memorandum :—'7. ' In the more recent treaty of 1837 it is stipulated that the solemn ' and paramount obligation provided by treaty for the prosperity ' of your Majesty's subjects, and the security of the lives and ' property of the inhabitants, has been notoriously neglected by ' several successive rulers in Oude, thereby exposing "the British ' " Government to the reproach of imperfectly fulfilling its obliga- ' " tions towards the Oude people ; " and accordingly his Majesty ' the King of Oude was bound to "take into his immediate and ' " earnest consideration, in concert with the Resident, the best ' " means of remedying the existing defects in the police, and in ' " the judicial and revenue administration ; and that if his Majesty ' " shall neglect to attend to the advice and counsel of the British ' " Government or its local representative, and if (which God ' " forbid) *gross and systematic oppression*, anarchy, and misrule ' " should hereafter at any time *prevail* within the Oude dominions, ' " such as seriously to endanger the public tranquillity, the British ' " Government reserves to itself the right of appointing its own ' " officers to manage whatsoever portions of territory, either great ' " or small, in which such misrule may have occurred, for so long a ' " period as it may deem necessary, the surplus receipts to be paid ' " into the King's Treasury."

' 8. I allude to the Treaty of 1837 as confirmatory of the ' original Treaty of 1801, which not only gave the British ' Government the right to interfere, but declared it to be the ' intention of the Government to interfere if necessary, for the ' purpose of securing good government in Oude.   .   .   .   .

' 12. These extracts will enable your Majesty to form a clear

by assuming the government of Oude. A period of two years was then fixed, as affording sufficient time for the correction of abuses, and the introduction of an amended system of administration.

The report of Colonel Sleeman, the British Resident at Lucknow, dated the 10th of December, 1851, contains a fearful account of the misgovernment of Oude, and the oppression of its people. The friendly disposition of this officer towards native States is well known, and yet he was compelled to write as follows :[1]—

'Fifty years of sad experience has shown, that 'the hopes in which the Treaty of 1801 was founded, 'that sovereigns of the reigning family of Oude 'would be disposed and able, to form and carry out, 'by means of their own officers, a system of 'administration calculated to secure life and pro- 'perty, to promote the welfare and happiness of 'the people of Oude, and to render the alliance

'judgment of the position in which the Kings of Oude are placed 'by treaty. The Governor-General is required, *when gross and* '*systematic abuses prevail*, to apply such a remedy as the exigency 'of the case may require ; he has no option in the performance 'of this duty.'

[1] Report of Colonel SLEEMAN, 10th December, 1851. Oude papers, p. 166.

' with the British Government, who were to protect
' those sovereigns from all foreign and domestic
' enemies, if not honourable to that Government,
' at least irreproachable, were altogether fallacious
' and can never be realized; and with a due regard
' to its own character, as the paramount power
' in India, and to the particular obligations by
' which it is bound by solemn treaties to the suffering
' people of this distracted country, I do not think
' that our Government can any longer forbear to
' exercise to the fullest extent, *the powers which the*
' *Treaty of* 1837 *confers upon it,* of taking upon itself
' the administration, and conducting it by means of
' their own officers.   .   .   .

    ' Numerous instances of all these evils and
' sufferings, and of the apathy with which they are
' viewed by the Oude government, are contained in
' the diaries which it is my duty to submit every
' month to Government, but they are not the
' tenth part of what every month takes place.   The
' Resident has every month to report flagrant
' instances of the same sort, after careful investiga-
' tion, for the consideration and orders of the
' Governor-General, all tending to show an utter
' disregard of the solemn duties imposed upon the

' sovereigns of Oude and their ministers by the
' treaties of 1801 and 1837.' It is clear from these
extracts, that the abrogation of the Treaty of 1837
was unknown to Colonel Sleeman — a fact also
apparent from his correspondence.[1]

In 1854, Lord Dalhousie's attention was called
to an authorized collection of the Treaties with native
states, printed at Calcutta in 1845, which contained
the disallowed Treaty of 1837. Lord Dalhousie
took immediate notice of this, and brought it before
his Council. Mr. Dorin then mentioned the fact,
that the abrogation of the treaty had never been
notified to the King, and this was confirmed by
Colonel Low (formerly Resident at Lucknow), who
assured the Council, that the disallowance of the
treaty had never been communicated to any one
at Lucknow, European or native.[2] Mr. Grant, the
third member of Council, recommended that the
King should, even at that late period, be informed
of the fact. The letter of the Governor-General in
Council, forwarding these Minutes, informed the

---

[1] See KAYE's *Sepoy War*, in note at p. 129.
[2] See all the Minutes on this subject ; Oude papers, ordered
to be printed 15th March, 1858, pp. 66, 67, 68.

Court, that the total abrogation of the Treaty had not been announced to the King of Oude, and that Lord Auckland had informed the Court of what he had done.[1] The Court of Directors, in their answer, did not refer to these facts, or attempt any explanation of them, but contented themselves with observing, ' that the best course was to take no step ' whatever, and to leave matters as they stood until ' some particular question arises, which must be ' dealt with according to circumstances.'[2]

The continued misgovernment of Oude, and the fearful state of that kingdom, at last forced themselves upon the attention of Lord Dalhousie.[3] In 1854, he felt obliged to take the very ominous course of directing Colonel Outram, then Resident at Lucknow, to report upon the state of the country, with a view of ascertaining whether its affairs continued to be in the same condition which

---

[1] Oude papers, ordered to be printed 15th March, 1858, p. 65.

[2] Letter of Court of Directors to Government of India, 10th January, 1855 ; Oude papers, ordered to be printed, 15th March, 1858, p. 68.

[3] He always entertained a great distaste for the subject. I remember a conversation with him in 1852, in which he stated that he had been pressed to take the country (by whom he did not say), and that he felt averse to such a measure. I cannot trust my memory to state the precise nature of his objections at that time.

former Residents described them to be, and whether the reform (for the accomplishment of which Lord Hardinge had given a period of two years,) had in any degree been effected. The report of Colonel Outram contained disclosures so frightful, that Lord Dalhousie was compelled to take up the consideration of the subject, with a view to its final decision.

Lord Dalhousie's Minute of the 18th of June, 1855, contains an elaborate history of our relations with Oude, and a full statement of the misgovernment of the country, and the wrongs of the people. Its argument is based on the Treaty of 1801, that of 1837 being null and void.[1] It acknowledges, as fully as could be expected from a Governor-General, the grave responsibility the British Government had incurred by allowing, for so long a period, such misrule in Oude. Thus he observes:[2]—' For tolerating so long this total ' disregard of the obligations of solemn Treaty, and ' for all the ills and human suffering which have ' sprung therefrom, the British Government is ' heavily responsible. It cannot, indeed, be

---

[1] Minute of 18th June, 1855 ; Oude papers, p. 149.
[2] Ibid. p. 180.

'charged with indifference to the evils whose
'existence it perceived, or with neglect of all
'exertions to palliate or remove them. For,
'from the date of the treaty to the present day,
'the records of Government exhibit one unbroken
'series of acts of counsel, of complaint, and of
'condemnation, on the part of the Government of
'India, and its representatives at Lucknow. By
'official notes, in friendly letters, through the
'mouth of the Resident, and at formal personal
'interviews, the Governor-General has urged,
'from time to time, upon the notice of the Ruler
'of Oude, the wretched internal condition of his
'kingdom; and, throughout all that period, at
'frequent intervals, words of indignant censure
'have alternated with earnest remonstrances, with
'warning, and with threats. But the Govern-
'ment of India has never taken the one measure
'which alone could be effectual, by withdrawing
'its countenance from the Sovereign of Oude,
'and its troops from his dominions. It is by
'these aids alone that the Sovereigns of Oude
'have been enabled for more than half-a-century
'to persist with impunity in their course of
'oppression and misrule. Their eyes have never

' seen the misery of their subjects ; their ears have
' never been open to their cry.   Secure of the
' safety of his person—secure of the stability of
' his throne—each successive ruler has passed his
' lifetime within the walls of his palace, or in the
' gardens round his capital, careful for nothing
' but the gratification of his individual passion—
' avarice, as in one ; intemperance, as in another ;
' or, as in the present King, effeminate sensuality,
' indulged among singers, musicians, and eunuchs,
' the sole companions of his confidence, and the
' sole agents of his power.   Were it not for the
' support which the Government of India is known
' to be bound to afford the King against all
' domestic as well as against foreign enemies ;
' were it not for the constant presence of British
' troops at Lucknow, the people of Oude would
' speedily work their own deliverance, and would
' impose upon their ruler the effectual check of
' general revolt by which Eastern rulers are best
' controlled.   Colonel Sleeman thus bears his
' testimony to this important truth : " I am per-
' " suaded," he says, " that, if our troops were
' " withdrawn from Oude, the landholders would
' " in one month march over them all, and pillage

' " the capital of Lucknow."   I respectfully sub-
' mit to the Honourable Court that the time has
' come when inaction on the part of the British
' Government, in relation to the affairs of the
' kingdom of Oude, can now be no longer justified,
' and is already converting our responsibility into
' guilt.'

Lord Dalhousie then observes that there were
four modes of proceeding : [1]—

'First, The King may be required to abdicate
' the sovereign powers he has abused, and to
' consent to the incorporation of Oude with the
' territories of the British Crown.

' Second, The King may be permitted to retain
' his royal title and position, but may be required
' to vest the whole civil and military administra-
' tion of his kingdom in the government of the
' East India Company for ever.

' Third, His Majesty may be urged to make
' over his dominions to the management of British
' officers for a time.

' Fourth, The King may be invited to place
' the management of the country in the hands of

---

[1] Paragraph 50, Minute of 18th June, 1855; Oude papers,
p. 184.

' the Resident ; under whose directions it shall be
' carried on by the officers of the King acting with
' such British officers as may be appointed to aid
' them.

' First, The King may be required to abdicate
' the sovereign powers he has abused, and to
' consent to the incorporation of Oude with the
' territories of the British Crown.

' Although the dynasty of Oude is a thing but
' of yesterday, sprung from treachery at the first,
' and only reared to kingly rank by ourselves, and
' although I firmly believe that the incorporation
' of that territory with the British dominions, and
' the bold extinction of its sovereignty, would be
' the happiest issue that could be desired for the
' interests of all connected with it, yet I do not
' counsel the adoption of that measure by the
' Government of India.

' The rulers of Oude, however unfaithful they
' may have been to the trust committed to them,
' however gross may have been their neglect,
' however grievous their misgovernment of the
' people committed to their charge, have yet ever
' been faithful and true in their adherence to the
' British power. No wavering friendship has ever

'been laid to their charge.   They have long
'acknowledged our power, have submitted with-
'out a murmur to our supremacy, and have aided
'us as best they could in the hour of our utmost
'need.   Wherefore, although we are bound to
'dissolve our connexion with a government whose
'oppression is sustained only by the countenance
'we lend it, and although we are entitled to
'seek by all means in our power to amend the
'lot of a people whom we have so long indirectly
'injured, justice and gratitude, nevertheless,
'require, that in so doing, we should lower the
'dignity and authority of the sovereigns of Oude,
'no further than is absolutely necessary for the
'accomplishment of our righteous ends.

'The reform of the administration of the pro-
'vince may be wrought, and the prosperity of the
'people may be secured, without resorting to so
'extreme a measure as the annexation of the
'territory, and the abolition of the throne.

'I, for my part, therefore, do not advise that
'the province of Oude should be declared to be
'British territory.'

The Minute then refers to the history of our
past relations with Oude, the Nizam, the Punjaub,

and Nagpore, as showing the inefficacy of a divided
government or a temporary assumption of power
(the second and third modes suggested), and thus
proceeds : [1]—

   ' It is my earnest counsel that no less effectual
' measure than that which is contained in the
' second project should be resolved upon, namely,
' that while the King should be permitted to retain
' his royal title and rank, he should be required
' to vest the whole civil and military adminis-
' tration of Oude in the hands of the Company,
' and that its power should be " perpetual in
' " duration, as well as ample in extent."

   ' It still remains to be considered in what
' manner the policy I have advocated may best
' be carried into effect.

   ' The King's consent is indispensable to the
' transfer of the whole or of any part of his
' sovereign authority to the government of the
' East India Company. It would not be expedient,
' or right, to endeavour to extract this consent by
' means of menace or compulsion. It must be
' sought by leading the King to perceive, that a
' simple regard for his own interests, and for the

---

[1] Oude papers, p. 187.

' maintenance of his family and throne, should
' of itself be sufficient to induce him to give
' his consent to those measures, which alone can
' save his kingdom and house from the misfortunes,
' which will surely follow his refusal to alter the
' course in which he has long unhappily persisted.

' In pursuance of this policy, I would propose
' that, as soon as the sanction of the Honourable
' Court shall be obtained to the necessary change
' in our relations with the Court of Lucknow, a
' letter should be addressed by the Governor-
' General to the King.' . . .

' The letter should proceed to state that the
' Resident had accordingly been directed to declare
' the treaty of 1801 at an end, to quit the territory
' of Oude, and to withdraw the entire subsidiary
' force within the British frontier.

' It should then be added that, as the King is
' well aware that his authority, and the very ex-
' istence of his throne, have long been maintained
' solely by the presence of a British force in Oude,
' his Majesty will readily foresee the consequences
' which would undoubtedly follow its withdrawal.
' If his Majesty is ready to meet those conse-
' quences, and to endure them, the Government

' of India will interpose no further in his Majesty's
' affairs, unless the security of its territories, and
' the interests of their inhabitants, shall be put in
' danger by the state of the neighbouring province
' of Oude. If, on the other hand, his Majesty
' should shrink from encountering those conse-
' quences, and should desire to avert them, his
' Majesty will have it in his power to do so by
' renewing relations of amity with the Govern-
' ment of India on conditions, which shall be calcu-
' lated to prevent a recurrence of misgovernment
' in Oude, while they will effectually secure the
' interests of his Majesty's family, and maintain
' his kingly rank in affluence and dignity.

' A draft treaty to the effect now stated should
' then be offered by the Resident to the King.'

Lord Dalhousie's Minute discloses a strong dis-
inclination to resort to extreme measures. What
his real opinions were will not be fully known
until his papers are published, for he was not one
to embarrass the action of Government by writing
hard things against his country, or making a case
for such creatures as the Kings of Oude. But a
careful examination of his Minutes has satisfied me,
that the conduct of the British Government towards

Oude, paralysed an arm never slow to adopt strong measures when right was on its side.

No doubt the Kings of Oude had failed to fulfil the obligations imposed on them by the Treaty of 1801. But for half a century, although we had remonstrated and threatened, we had done nothing to enforce their observance of the treaty, and our long acquiescence had verged on a participation of their guilt.[1] We had placed them in a position in which good government was impossible, and Lord Dalhousie laid particular stress, as we shall presently see, on one of the provisions of the Treaty of 1801, which had in itself frustrated all the good intentions of its framers.[2] And, lastly, the sovereigns of Oude, with all their faults, had been our faithful and useful allies.[3]

No doubt the Treaty of 1837 was null and void, but we had concealed from the King the disallowance of that Treaty, and had allowed him to suppose that the worst that could befall him was the temporary administration of Oude by our officers, leav-

---

[1] See extracts from Lord Dalhousie's Minute, *ante*, pp. 181, 184.

[2] Minute of 13th February, 1856, para. 15; Oude papers, 299. See *post*, p. 152.

[3] See extract from Lord Dalhousie's Minute, *ante*, pp. 185, 186.

ing him in possession of the throne and surplus revenues. Although this concealment could not operate so as to give effect to a Treaty which was in fact null and void, yet it might.deter a Governor-General from inflicting a more severe penalty than the disallowed Treaty imposed; and if the infliction of that penalty was for any reason unadvisable, surely fair dealing required, that we should abstain from force, wash our hands as clean as we could of all our transactions with Oude, and begin a new career unfettered by the past. That considerations of this nature did affect Lord Dalhousie to some extent, will presently appear.

Lord Dalhousie's proposal for a return to the *statu quo ante* was not without its difficulties, for the Treaty bound us to secure good government for the people of Oude, and our proposed departure would be followed by a continuance of misrule. But Lord Dalhousie thought, that the King's fear of the vengeance which his own subjects would exact if he were left alone, would induce him to sign the Treaty; and if not, the withdrawal of the British troops would be the signal for such an insurrection, as would induce the King, within a month, to agree to whatever stipulations might be offered to him

by the British Government.[1]　It was also the
opinion of Colonel Low, that our departure would
be followed by insurrections which would compel
our return.[2] If such events had occurred we should
then have been unfettered by Treaties, and able to
do what we thought best for the people of Oude.

There was yet another difficulty in Lord Dalhousie's proposed return to the *statu quo ante*, inasmuch as he did not intend to restore to the Kings
of Oude the territory made over to us by the Treaty
of 1801, as a compensation for a subsidy which was
then determined, and as the consideration for the
future assistance we had agreed to give the King
against foreign and domestic enemies.　No doubt
Lord Dalhousie felt, that we had been in possession
of this territory more than fifty years, that third
parties, the inhabitants of these territories, had now
acquired rights under that treaty, and that the
British Government had also incurred obligations
as the ruler of those territories, and that these
rights and obligations could not be lightly resigned
to such a Government as that of Oude.　But these

---

[1] See Minute of 18th February, 1856 ; Oude papers, 299, 300.

[2] Minute of Col. (now Major Sir John) Low ; Oude papers,
pp. 221, 222.

considerations do not remove the difficulty; they only show more clearly, how impossible it was to return to the *statu quo ante*, and that the utmost Lord Dalhousie could do, would only produce such an approximation to the former relations between the parties, as existing circumstances permitted.

The recommendations of Lord Dalhousie were not approved of by the Members of his Council. Mr. Dorin advised annexation and the deposition of the King, and Mr. Grant [1] was of the same opinion, except that he would have allowed the King to retain his title during his life. Mr. Grant contended, in his very able Minute, that ever since the Treaty of 1801, if not before, the British Government had been in fact the rulers of Oude, governing it by means of a dependent King, who had bound himself by treaty to govern well, and that the King, having failed to fulfil his engagement, it was the duty of the British Government to remove him. Mr. Peacock,[2] considering the King a protected, rather

---

[1] Now Sir John P. Grant, K.C.B.

[2] Now Sir Barnes Peacock, the Chief Justice of the High Court at Calcutta.

than a dependent, sovereign, insisted that his violation of the Treaty by the oppression of the people, justified the British Government in resorting to such force as was necessary to secure good government, and that the permanent assumption of the government of the country, without depriving the King and his posterity of their rank as sovereigns, was all that was necessary. Colonel Low, also, supported this view, and it was urged by all the Council, with more or less force, that if the British Government felt the wrongs of the people of Oude so strongly, as to interfere on their behalf under the Treaty of 1801, they would be acting inconsistently, and at the same time unjustly, if they annulled the Treaty, quitted the country, and left its people without redress.

On the arrival of these Minutes in England, the Cabinet were consulted, and in accordance with their advice, the Court of Directors issued their final orders for the assumption of the government of Oude. Their despatch of the 21st of November, 1855, is a specimen of the art of writing important instructions so as to avoid responsibility, but it expresses their disapproval of Lord Dalhousie's plan of obtaining the free consent of the King to a new

Treaty, and in case of his refusal, of cancelling the Treaty of 1801, and withdrawing from Oude ; and it directs that unless it was 'the conviction of the 'Governor-General' that the King's alarm at such a threat would render his acceptance of the Treaty 'a matter of virtual certainty,' that alternative should not be offered to him; and it authorizes 'the only other course by which our duties to the 'people of Oude can be fulfilled—that of assuming 'authoritatively the powers necessary for the per- 'manent establishment of good government through- 'out the country, leaving all questions of detail to 'the wisdom of the Governor-General, in con- 'junction with the other members of your govern- 'ment.' The Court of Directors, in fact, supported the opinions of the members of Council against that of the Governor-General.

Some men, under such circumstances, would have gladly shifted the burden of annexation on that Council, and on that new Governor-General, now slowly approaching the shores of India, who, as a member of the English Cabinet, had advised it. But Lord Dalhousie had some time before written to the Court of Directors, expressing his belief, that it would be more advantageous for the public service, that he

10

should deal with this question than a new Governor-General, first entering on his government ; and the Court now availed themselves of this offer, and observed : ' It is in every account to be desired that ' the great measure which we have authorized ' should be carried into effect under the auspices of ' the nobleman, who has so long, and with such ' eminent ability and success, administered the affairs ' of the British Empire in India, who has bestowed ' such attention and earnest consideration on this ' particular subject, and whose acts may carry a ' weight of authority which might, perhaps, not in ' the same degree attach to the first proceedings of ' a new administration.' [1]

Lord Dalhousie, although he was now ill, and scarcely able to walk, was the last man to shrink from the fulfilment of any offer he had made, and he now resolved, with a spirit of self-sacrifice, to take upon himself the odium of this annexation, —a measure which he foretold would bring him no credit, and would be violently assailed by the opponents of the Indian Government.[2] And thus

---

[1] Oude papers, p. 236.

[2] Lord Dalhousie's letter to Court of Directors, 3rd July, 1855. Oude papers, p. 1.

Oude came to be annexed by the statesman, who had alone opposed the adoption of that course.

The private instructions prepared by Lord Dalhousie for Colonel Outram's guidance, during the discussions expected to take place when he should announce the orders of government to the King, show us more of Lord Dalhousie's inmost thoughts with respect to our relations with Oude, than he thought fit to disclose in his Minute. These instructions contain the following remarkable passage :[1]—

' It is very probable that the King, in the course
' of the discussions which will take place with the
' Resident, may refer to the treaty negotiated with
' his predecessor in 1837.[2] The Resident is aware
' that that treaty was not continued in force, having
' been annulled by the Court of Directors so soon
' as it was received in England. The Resident is
' further aware, that although the King of Oude was

---

[1] Oude papers, p. 239.

[2] The King was overwhelmed by the announcement of his fate, and wholly incapable of argument, but it appears from the letter he sent to the Resident on the 1st of February, 1856, that he insisted that our conduct was at variance with the ' Treaties,'— there being only two Treaties in existence, those of 1801 and 1837. Oude papers, p. 288.

' informed at that time that certain provisions of
' the Treaty of 1837, respecting an increased mili-
' tary force, would not be carried into effect, the
' entire abrogation of the Treaty by the Court of
' Directors was never communicated to his Majesty.

' *The effect of this reserve and want of full com-*
' *munication is felt to be embarrassing to this day.*
' It is the more embarrassing that the cancelled
' instrument was still included in a volume of
' treaties which was published in 1845, by the
' authority of Government. *There is no better way*
' *of encountering this difficulty than by meeting it*
' *full in the face.*

' If the King should allude to the Treaty of
' 1837, and should ask why, if further measures
' are necessary in relation to the administration
' of Oude, the large powers which are given to
' the British Government by the said Treaty should
' not now be put in force, his Majesty must be
' informed that the Treaty has had no existence
' since it was communicated to the Court of Di-
' rectors, by whom it was wholly annulled. His
' Majesty will be reminded that the Court of
' Lucknow was informed at the time that certain
' articles of the Treaty of 1837, by which the

' payment of an additional military force was
' imposed on the King, were to be set aside. It
' must be presumed, that it was not thought neces-
' sary at that time to make any communication
' to his Majesty regarding those articles of the
' Treaty which were not of immediate operation,
' and that a subsequent communication was un-
' doubtedly neglected. *The Resident will be at*
' *liberty to state that the Governor-General in Council*
' *regrets that any such neglect should have taken place,*
' *even inadvertently.* The Resident may at the same
' time observe that the absence of a final communi-
' cation to the Court of Lucknow, regarding the
' annulment of the Treaty of 1837 by the Govern-
' ment of that day, has not been productive of any
' detriment whatever to his Majesty's interests,
' either then or at any later period.

' Should his Majesty observe, that although the
' Treaty of 1837 was annulled, and is no longer in
' existence, a similar measure less stringent than
' that which is now proposed, might be adopted
' on the present occasion, his Majesty should be
' requested to observe, that the measure to which
' he refers was at once rejected by the Supreme
' Authorities in England ; and that all subsequent

' experience has shown, that the remedy which
' the Treaty of 1837 supplied, would be wholly
' inadequate to remove the evils and abuses, which
' have long marked the condition of Oude.'

These instructions have led me to conclude, that
Lord Dalhousie's proposal for a return to the *statu
quo ante*, was partly the result of the embarrassment
and difficulty raised in his mind by our concealment
of the abrogation of the Treaty from the King.
The Treaty of 1837 was void,—its provisions
incapable of being conceded as a matter of grace,
—and therefore he proposed a return to the *statu
quo ante*.

On the 13th of February, 1856, after the
annexation had taken place, and just before Lord
Dalhousie's departure, he recorded another Minute
on this subject.   It manifests an undiminished
preference for that course, which he had suggested
in his former Minute and had been obliged to
abandon.   He observes,[1] ' I considered it to be my
' duty to suggest, not the mode of proceeding
' which might seem to be the shortest and the
' easiest for the Government of India, but that

---

[1] Oude Papers, p. 299.

' mode of proceeding, which, while it should be
' effectual for the purpose designed, should at the
' same time be in most accordance with established
' usage and most in conformity *to international*
' *law, and therefore least liable to criticism or cavil,*
' and least open to the attack of those who might
' be expected to condemn and oppose the measure.
' . . . It was not for me to suggest for the
' adoption of the Honourable Court in the first
' instance, and without necessity, any line of
' political action which was likely to create a
' keener opposition *and to call forth severer*
' *comment*, than would be elicited by adherence
' to the usual course of action which public law
' and settled custom had prescribed.

' Acting upon this view of my duty, I con-
' sidered that it was open to me to advise that the
' fulfilment of the Treaty of 1801 should be com-
' pelled by force of arms, or that the treaty should
' be declared null and void, by reason of the con-
' tinuous violation of it by the rulers of Oude.

' The former alternative, which has been
' advocated by Mr. Peacock, was rejected by me,
' and has been in like manner rejected by the
' Honourable Court, as neutralized in this par-

' ticular case, and rendered insufficient to secure
' the object at which we are aiming, by the pecu-
' liar provisions of the Treaty of 1801.

' " By those treaties," the Honourable Court
' observed, " the king of Oude is bound, in general
' " terms, to govern according to the advice of the
' " Residents, and specifically to introduce into his
' " territory a reformed system of administration.
' " But it also provided that this reformed system
' " shall be carried into effect by his own officers ;
' " and throughout the period of more than half-
' " a-century, during which the treaties have
' " existed, *this one provision has frustrated all the*
' " *efforts that have been made to induce the sovereigns*
' " *of Oude to fulfil their obligations to the British*
' " *Government and their own subjects.*" [1]

' The alternative of compelling the fulfilment
' of the Treaty by force of arms being thus closed
' against us by the peculiar provisions of the treaty
' itself, I feel myself bound to advise that the
' Treaty of 1801 should be declared null and
' void, that our troops should be withdrawn,

---

[1] The italics here are those of Lord Dalhousie himself. I have
referred to the argument founded on this provision of the Treaty
of 1801, *ante*, pp. 121, 122.

'that our protection of the government should
'cease, and that all our relations with it should
'be broken off.

'I have never affected to conceal my convic-
'tion that this measure would lead to precisely
'the same result as the more peremptory course
'advised by others, but with some intervening
'delay. . . .

'Holding firmly to these views of the expe-
'diency of guiding our political action in relation
'to Oude by established law and custom, and
'finding no weight in the objections to the course
'which had already been advised, I should have
'preferred to act on the suggestions which were
'originally submitted to the Honourable Court in
'my Minute of the 18th of June.

'But the sentiments of my colleagues were
adverse,' &c.

Lord Dalhousie's own scheme for the withdrawal of the British forces from Oude, in the
event of the King's refusing his assent to a new
treaty, having been disallowed, only one of three
courses remained open to him,—first, he might
annex Oude, deposing the King; secondly, he

might assume the government of the country permanently, recognizing the King as its nominal sovereign with a fixed pension; and, thirdly, he might assume the government of the country permanently, recognizing the King as its actual sovereign, and making the British Government accountable to him for the surplus revenues.

Mr. Kaye thinks the last alternative should have been adopted. But it is not easy to see wherein such an arrangement differed in principle from that proposed by Lord Auckland in the Treaty of 1837, which was peremptorily disallowed by the Home Government; and there is certainly no ground for saying that the Home Government of 1856, was likely to be more favourable to such an arrangement than that of 1837. The objections, however, to this course are patent, and have been well stated by Lord Dalhousie, as follows :— [1]

' The Government of India would not be ' justified in making over such a surplus to the ' reigning sovereign of Oude, only that it might ' be unprofitably wasted by him, and squandered ' upon the follies, and excesses, and vices, which

---

[1] See his Minute of 18th June, 1855; Oude papers, pp. 189, 190.

' are the usual characteristics of a native prince.
' . . . If the Government of India shall not only
' renew its former obligations to defend the King
' from all foreign and domestic enemies, but shall
' undertake new and onerous duties, in addition to
' them; if it shall consent to bear henceforth all
' the labour, all the risk, of reconstructing and
' permanently administering the Government of
' Oude, and of supplying the numerous European
' agency which will be required for the purpose,
' surely it may justly covenant that after fully
' providing for the pensioned dynasty of Oude,
' for the administration of the province, and for
' its progressive improvement, the Supreme Govern-
' ment shall be at liberty to devote to the general
' advantage of the Indian Empire some portion. of
' that surplus of the revenue of Oude, of which
' our own exertions and resources shall have been
' the sole origin and creative cause.'

If it be said, that the difficulty arising from the
non-communication of the disallowance of the
Treaty of 1837 was a reason, more or less impe-
rative, for the adoption of this course, it may well
be said, that of all concerned, Lord Dalhousie's
Government was the least responsible for that

difficulty. . I have shown that they pressed upon the Home Government, in 1854, the propriety of removing it, by a formal communication to the King ; but were not permitted to do so. Lord Dalhousie felt that the Treaty of 1837 was null and void ; that any scheme involving a similar policy would not receive the sanction of the authorities which had rejected that Treaty,[1] and that the scheme was objectionable in itself.

The first course I have suggested as being open to Lord Dalhousie—that of annexing Oude and deposing its King—he would not adopt, for the reasons set forth in his Minute of the 18th of June, 1855.[2]

The only course, therefore, that remained was that which was actually adopted. A new treaty was offered for the King's signature, transferring the government of his country permanently to the East India Company, but recognizing the King as a nominal sovereign, with a large pension for himself and his heirs. On his refusal to sign this Treaty, the government of Oude was permanently assumed by the British authorities, leaving the *status* of

---

[1] See instructions to Colonel Outram, *ante*, p. 149.
[2] See *antc*, pp. 185, 186.

the King and his family for subsequent arrangement.[1]

My object in investigating these transactions is
fully answered, if I have shown that Lord Dalhousie
was not possessed of the dominant passion for
annexation which has been so unjustly imputed to
him ; that he was in fact opposed to the annexation
of Oude; that the responsibility of that measure
rests, not with him, but with the English Cabinet
and the Court of Directors ; and that his part in the
transaction was the last sacrifice which he made on
the altar of duty.

---

[1] Lord Dalhousie granted the King a pension of 120,000*l.* a
year.

MILITARY PROPOSALS.

When the Mutiny broke upon us in 1857, with a small European force wholly unequal to the task of repressing it, it was natural that the public should seek for some one to blame, and matters were so ingeniously managed, that the blame eventually settled on Lord Dalhousie, who had left India fifteen months before the Mutiny began, who had protested against the reduction of the European force which took place in his time, and had recommended a very considerable increase to that force, as well as a large reduction of the native army.

Mr. Kaye observes,[1]—' If anything should teach ' us the wisdom of never suffering our European ' force, even in the most tranquil times, to decline

---

[1] Kaye's *Sepoy War*, p. 341.

' below what we may call " the athletic standard,"
' it is the fact, that when the times cease to be
' tranquil, we cannot suddenly raise it to the
' standard without exciting alarm and creating dan-
' ger. But this lesson was not learnt. Or, *if Indian*
' *statesmen ever took it to their hearts*, it was remorse-
' lessly repudiated in the council of the English
' nation.' An examination of what took place, will
enable us to assign to this remark its proper place and
value, in a history of Lord Dalhousie's administration.

In 1854, during the Crimean war, the Home
authorities proposed to withdraw two of her Majesty's
infantry regiments (the 25th and 98th) from India.
Lord Dalhousie objected to this,[1] in a forcible
Minute, dated the 13th of September, 1854, from
which I shall cite two passages. The first passage
is prophetic of some of the events which followed :[2]—

' We are perfectly secure so long as we are
' strong, and are believed to be so ; but if European
' troops shall now be withdrawn from India to
' Europe, if countenance shall thus be given to the
' belief, already prevalent, that we have grappled

---

[1] He had already sent two Cavalry regiments to the Crimea.

[2] Parliamentary papers ordered to be printed by House of
Commons in 1858.

' with an antagonist whose strength will prove equal
' to overpower us, if by consenting to withdrawal,
' we shall weaken that essential element of our
' military strength, which has already been declared
' to be no more than adequate for ordinary times,
' and if, further, we should be called on to despatch
' an army to the Persian Gulf, an event which,
' unlooked for now, may any day be brought about
' by the thraldom in which Persia is held, and by
' the feeble and fickle character of the Shah; then,
' indeed, I shall no longer feel, and can no longer
' express, the same confidence as before, that the
' security and stability of our position in the East
' will remain unassailed.'

The second passage shows, that Lord Dalhousie
did not overlook the consequences of that increase
in our dominions, which the narrative of Mr. Kaye
implies to have been the discovery of 'intelligent
' natives.'[1]　Speaking of the distances at which
the European regiments were stationed from each
other, Lord Dalhousie observes:[2]—' I confidently
' submit to the candour of her Majesty's Ministers,

---

[1] KAYE's *Sepoy War*, pp. 343, 844.

[2] Minute, 13th September, 1854.　Parliamentary Papers
ordered to be printed on motion of Mr. Vansittart in 1858.

' that placed as it is amidst distances so vast, amidst
' multitudes so innumerable, amidst people and
' sects various in many things, but all alike in this,
' that they are lately conquered subjects of our race,
' alien to them in religion, language, in colour, in
' habits, in all feelings and interests, the Govern-
' ment of India has had solid grounds for the
' declaration, *more than once made of late years*, that
' the European force at its command is not more
' than adequate for preserving the empire in security
' and tranquillity, even in ordinary times, much
' more then,' &c.

Notwithstanding this remonstrance, her Majesty's 25th and 98th regiments were withdrawn from India, without relief, reducing the number of Royal regiments of Infantry to twenty-two, and not twenty-four, as stated by Mr. Kaye.[1] Although this was said to be a mere temporary arrangement, occasioned by the drain on our resources at that time, and although the nominal establishment of Infantry for India remained at thirty-three battalions,[2] the two battalions thus withdrawn were not replaced at the

---

[1] KAYE'S *Sepoy War*, p. 841.

[2] See Lord Dalhousie's Minute (No. 2) on European Infantry, 5th February, 1856. Parliamentary Papers ordered to be printed in 1858.

11

end of the Crimean war, and when the Mutiny broke out, there were only thirty-one battalions of European Infantry actually on the Indian establishment,[1] and five or six of these were absent in that Persian war, which Lord Dalhousie had foreseen.

On the 28th of February, 1856, the last day Lord Dalhousie presided at the Council of India, he laid on its table nine Minutes, containing his views and proposals on military subjects.   He requested that they might be forthwith transmitted to the Home authorities, a request which was complied with the next day.   I cannot find that any further attention was paid to these Minutes, either at home or in India.   Nothing more was heard of them, until the year 1858, when, in consequence of a motion of Mr. Vansittart's in the House of Commons, one of them (No. 2), and also the Minute of the 13th of September, 1854, already referred to, were produced and printed.   I know

---

[1] There were nine regiments of European (Company's) Infantry, and the following Royal Infantry regiments, twenty-two in number, viz., the 8th, 10th, 24th, 27th, 29th, 32nd, 35th, 43rd, 52nd, 53rd, 60th—1st battalion, 61st, 64th, 70th, 74th, 75th, 78th, 81st, 83rd, 84th, 86th, 87th.   In all, thirty-one battalions.

not on what grounds the other eight Minutes were withheld, but their suppression, coupled with articles, which appeared at the time in the public prints, misstating their effect, grievously affected Lord Dalhousie's reputation. Even now, it is impossible to state the full effect of these Minutes; for although the authorities at the India House, including Mr. Kaye himself, rendered me every assistance, two of them are not to be found, and I have been obliged to collect as much as possible of their effect, (but whether or not the whole, I am unable to say,) from references to them in the other Minutes.

Minute No. 1 (missing) proposed the raising of two European Cavalry regiments for the Company's service in Bengal,—the officers for these regiments· being taken from four regular regiments of native Cavalry, which were to be disbanded. As Lord Dalhousie suggested the withdrawal of the two Royal regiments of Cavalry in Bengal, this proposal would not have increased the European force, although it would have greatly reduced the regular native Cavalry, which afterwards proved to be unfaithful.

Minutes Nos. 2 and 3 refer to the European

Infantry, and propose to raise the establishment from thirty-three, its nominal, and thirty-one, its actual number of battalions, to thirty-five battalions, and if possible to thirty-seven battalions. The force of thirty-five battalions, Lord Dalhousie proposed to get by replacing in Bengal the two Royal regiments withdrawn during the Crimean war, and by raising two more regiments of Company's European Infantry, one for each of the presidencies of Bengal and Madras, disbanding two native regiments in each of those presidencies to obtain officers for such new European corps. In paragraph 19 he says,—' I mention nineteen battalions as the *mini-* ' *mum* force of European infantry which ought to ' be maintained on the Bengal establishment— ' twenty battalions would be better, and even more ' would not be superfluous ;' and if Lord Dalhousie had adverted to the approaching annexation of Oude, when he signed this Minute,[1] he would have altered

---

[1] The Minute is dated on the 5th of February, 1856, only two days before the annexation, in the hurry of business preceding Lord Dalhousie's departure, but it bears internal evidence that it was written some time before its date, inasmuch as it assigns troops to specified places, and assigns none to Oude, though European troops were actually there on the 5th of February, to support the Resident if necessary.

this suggestion into a positive demand for a still greater increase. The Minute proposes, that if the European force is increased to thirty-seven battalions of Infantry according to his suggestion, the two additional battalions should also be Company's regiments, one for Bengal and one for Madras, the officers for them being obtained by disbanding two more native regiments in each presidency.

No. 4 Minute recommends the removal of the European Invalid Companies stationed at Chunar, where they were useless, to some other place where they might add to the apparent military strength.

No. 5 is missing, but I found the following passage in Minute 8 or 9 referring to it :—'The ' augmentation of European companies of Artillery ' which was solicited by the Commandant, has ' already been proposed by me in one of the series of ' Minutes on military establishments, which is now ' before my colleagues. The augmentation, however, ' was proposed in the form of companies, not of ' a battalion, and I prefer to adhere to that pro- ' posal.' It is clear, therefore, that he proposed an increase in the European companies of Artillery, though the amount of the increase cannot now be ascertained.

Minute 6 contains Lord Dalhousie's proposals
for the Bengal native Infantry. There were
seventy-four regular regiments, and two of these
being disbanded to obtain the officers for the
new European regiment, he proposed to reduce the
remaining seventy-two regiments from 1,000 to
800 Sepoys, with a corresponding deduction of
non-commissioned officers (say ten) in each corps.
He proposed that the three irregular Ghoorka
regiments should be raised from 640 to 800 men
each, and that those corps and the 66th native regiment (also Ghoorkas) should be armed with rifles,
and that four irregular regiments of native Infantry,
of 800 men each, should be raised for particular
service in the Punjaub. In other words, he proposed to strengthen the Ghoorka force ;[1] to reduce
the regular native infantry by 14,910 men ;[2] and
to increase the irregular native infantry by 3,200
men ; thus effecting a total reduction of about
11,710 Sepoys.

---

[1] Increase in the three Irregular Ghoorka Regiments, 480
men ; reduction in 66th Ghoorkas, 200 men : increase, 280 men.

[2] As the 66th were not Sepoys, but Ghoorkas, they should be
excluded from the reduction. This leaves 71 regiments to be
reduced by 210 men, that is, 14,910 men.

Minute No. 7 treats of the Bengal native Cavalry. The regular Cavalry of that presidency consisted of ten regiments, but four of these being disbanded, and their officers transferred to the new European Cavalry regiments, under Minute No. 1, Lord Dalhousie proposed to reduce the six remaining regiments from 420 to 300 troopers. This effected a reduction of 2,400 native troopers.[1] He also proposed, that all the Irregular Cavalry regiments (24 in number) should be reduced from 500 to 400 troopers. This reduction, however, was almost neutralized by another proposal to raise four additional regiments of irregular Cavalry for particular service in the Punjaub.[2]

Another Minute proposed the addition of two additional lieutenants to each regiment, with the view of meeting the great demand for officers for the. Staff and Irregular regiments. This recommendation, as it involved some patronage, appears to have been attended to, and improved upon, for,

---

[1] Four regular regiments of native Cavalry disbanded, 1,680; six regiments of native cavalry reduced by 120 men each, 720; number reduced, 2,400.

[2] The reduction in the irregular Cavalry would be 2,400; increase of four new regiments, 1,600. Total reduction, 800 men.

shortly afterwards, a captain and lieutenant were added to each corps.

Lastly, Lord Dalhousie proposed that the Commissariat department should be separated from the regimental strength, and should be constituted a separate Staff department by itself. This suggestion, neglected at the time, was probably the origin of that Staff Corps, which has now been established in India.

I will only say a few words as to these recommendations of Lord Dalhousie. It requires no military science to estimate the value of four more battalions of European infantry at the commencement of the Mutiny. With one of them at Cawnpore, another at Lucknow, and the two newly-raised corps doing duty in such garrisons as Forts William and St. George, thus freeing other regiments for active service, it is probable that the rebellion might have been at once repressed, or its progress might have been delayed, and its extent limited, so as to save many valuable lives and avert much subsequent difficulty. And those who know what the weak European companies of Artillery (only 90 men) had to go through at Cawnpore, Lucknow, Indore, and elsewhere, during the Mutiny, will fully appreciate the proposed increase in their strength. But to form a just opinion of Lord Dalhousie's proposal for the increase of the European force, it must be considered in connection with that large decrease of the native army which he also proposed—a reduction which greatly increased the relative proportion of the two forces.

With whom the blame rests of neglecting these recommendations I know not, nor do I care to know. My object is not to throw blame on any one, but to rescue Lord Dalhousie from the charge of leaving India, without having considered our military position in that country, and without having taken due precautions for its improvement.

I know not on what authority Mr. Kaye speaks of Lord Dalhousie's ' rooted conviction of the fidelity ' of the sepoy.[1] ' The extract referred to by Mr. Kaye on that point in the Farewell Minute, is part of a section which treats of the material condition of the army. Speaking of the European part of it, he mentions the improvement in their barracks, food, and health, and adverting to the Sepoy he says,[2]

---

[1] KAYE's *Sepoy War*, p. 324, and see 203.

[2] *Ibid.* p. 203, and Lord Dalhousie's Farewell Minute.

' Hardly any circumstance of his condition is in need of
' improvement'—an observation exclusively directed
to his physical condition, and not to his loyalty.   In
the absence of any unfavourable reports from the
military authorities, or of any facts calculated to
excite alarm, Lord Dalhousie must have been
omniscient, if he could have foreseen a mutiny, which
originated in greased cartridges unknown to the
Sepoy in his time.   What he thought of the Sepoy
must be, to some extent, a matter of conjecture, but
his recorded Minutes insist on the European force
as ' the essential element of our strength,' [1] and his
military proposals suggest an increase in our
European, and a decrease in our native army.

---

[1] Minute of 13th September, 1854, *ante*, p. 160.

CONCLUSION.

———◆———

It may be rash to speculate on future opinion, but I am confident, that when the history of Lord Dalhousie's administration is impartially written, the propriety of his annexations will be gratefully acknowledged. It will then appear, that he duly appreciated the responsibility cast upon him by the public law of India, and properly refused to recreate the extinct dynasties of Sattarah, Jhansi, Nagpore, and Sumbulpore, thereby consolidating our empire, and securing a good government for the population of those States. It will then be admitted that other causes than annexation excited that rebellion in Jhansi and Sumbulpore, which annexation did not produce in Nagpore and Sattarah.

That history will record, how, on the restoration of peace in the Punjaub, Lord Dalhousie swept away one of those dependent double Governments, in which the old Anglo-Indian school of politicians delighted to trust, and having annexed that province, administered its Government so wisely and so well, that when our hour of trial came, the subjugated race not only remained faithful, but proved our best allies in the suppression of rebellion elsewhere. The page that relates the conquest and annexation of Pegu, will also mention, that under the administration of that province, organized by Lord Dalhousie, the population was so satisfied with our rule, that when the mutiny burst out, the European garrison, with the exception of a few companies, was safely withdrawn, and sent on service elsewhere. When the clamour of paid advocacy has ceased, the wisdom and foresight of Lord Dalhousie, in refusing to recognize any longer, such rallying points for the disaffected as the titular sovereignties of the Carnatic and Tanjore, will be gratefully acknowledged; and although history will narrate, that his hand signed the proclamation annexing the kingdom of Oude, it will also record the fact, that of all the statesmen of his time, Lord Dalhousie was the least responsible for that measure.

The administration of Lord Dalhousie was the commencement of a new era in India, and her great advance in civilization will date from the time of his government. Under his rule large sums were for the first time set aside for Public Works. The Grand Trunk Road was continued from Delhi throughout the Punjaub, and other great lines of road were constructed. The Baree Dooab, and Ganges Canals, and other public works in Madras, provided for the irrigation of large districts. The Anna Postage and Electric Telegraph established throughout the country, and the system of Railroads, devised and commenced by Lord Dalhousie, secured for India that cheap and frequent interchange of thought, and rapidity of communication, which will add to her happiness, and promote her civilization. Measures taken for the suppression of female infanticide, and the Meriah sacrifices, large grants for educational purposes, and Lord Dalhousie's personal support of the late Mr. Bethune's school for the education of native girls, attest his anxiety for the moral improvement of the native population.

And not content with the present, but looking carefully into the future, he imported, from England and elsewhere, men of skill and science, and employed them in exploring the mineral and other resources of the vast empire he governed.

Momentous events occurred, and great questions were decided during the eight years of Lord Dalhousie's administration. He spared no labour in coming to a right conclusion on all of them, and, whether right or wrong, he adduced weighty reasons for every act of his administration. Those reasons convinced most men at the time, and public opinion approved, and applauded, his whole policy. But the tide has now turned, and because, more than a year after he left India, the mutiny and rebellion broke out, it has occurred to ingenious minds to suggest, that they were the consequences of Lord Dalhousie's policy. Every act of his administration has been canvassed with the view of extracting from it some cause, proximate or remote, of rebellion; and even the railroad and electric wire have been introduced into a picture,[1] worked up with all a painter's skill, to show the discontent produced by his Government.

---

[1] KAYE's *Sepoy War*, p. 190.

No impartial historian can attribute the mutiny, or the subsequent rebellion, to Lord Dalhousie's administration. In his time the greased cartridges, which are now admitted to have been the proximate cause of the mutiny, were unknown to the Sepoy, and there would have been no rebellion if there had not been a mutiny. The mutiny and the circumstances attending its outbreak convinced every native in India, that our Sepoys were disaffected, and that we were weak in the essential element of our military power—European soldiers. This knowledge, confirmed by the unchecked success of the mutineers for a time, was quite sufficient to excite rebellion in subjugated races, differing from us in colour, habits, and religion, and loving us not. The mutiny stirred native society to its lowest depths. The Hindoo sympathized with the fancied wrongs of the Sepoy. The Mohammedan thought the time was come to assert once more the supremacy of his religion and race. The disaffected throughout India felt that our power was shaken, and that the time to strike for freedom was come. It may be, that, when rebellion took courage from the mutiny, and burst forth into action, it betrayed the existence of discontent, and the old antagonism between darkness and light, but the discontent was that of subjugated races—the antagonism was that of ignorance and falsehood opposed to civilization and truth.

I shall not follow the example set me by recent publications, and attempt a description of Lord Dalhousie's character. I feel unequal to such a task, although I would say a few words, in conclusion, on the character which others have given him.

It seems almost superfluous to object to those descriptions of Lord Dalhousie, which characterize him as possessed of ' one dominant passion ' which drove him ' beyond the boundaries of conventional ' justice, generosity, and good faith,'[1] as taking ' a sheriff's officer's advantage of the Nizam,' ' as ' resorting to a technicality of the law courts,' ' to ' deprive the Ranee of Tanjore of her crown and ' treasure,'[2] and as being ' the worst and basest of ' rulers.'[3] These remarks might have been ex-

---

[1] ARNOLD's *Dalhousie Administration*, vol. ii. p. 200.

[2] For these and other similar passages, see vol. ii. of ARNOLD's *Dalhousie Administration*, pp. 199, 200.

[3] *The Empire in India*, by Major BELL, Madras Staff Corps, p. 26.

cusable, if Lord Dalhousie had done his great deeds to aggrandize his own fortune; but when it is remembered that all his acts were done in the service of his country, that weighty reasons were assigned for all of them, and that, whether right or wrong, they were all done with the view of benefiting this country as well as India, and as such, received the sanction of his Sovereign, her Ministers, and Parliament, the unprejudiced mind revolts from such language, as extravagant and unjustifiable.

Mr. Kaye says Lord ' Dalhousie had no imagina- ' tion,' and that for want of that faculty he was unable to sympathize with those under his rule.[1] It may be that he was unable to form ' a dramatic ' conception of the feelings ' of ' the representative ' of a long line of kings,' or ' of the greybeard ' chief,' mentioned by Mr. Kaye, but I doubt whether a man with his almost intuitive power of appreciating the men around him, could be totally destitute of imagination. Whether he did, or did not, possess that faculty, he possessed other qualities essential to a Governor, unrivalled

---

[1] KAYE's *Sepoy War*, pp. 856, 857.

12

powers of perception, and an anxious desire to be right on every occasion—a desire which led him to investigate with such labour, and discuss with such logical precision, all the great questions that came before him. Some may prefer a Governor with a lively imagination, but I must confess to a preference for qualities, rarely found in combination with great imaginative powers,—care, accuracy, common sense, and a sound judgment.

As to Lord Dalhousie's supposed want of sympathy for those under his rule, I do not think an adverse opinion as to his annexations justifies so severe a reflection on his memory. Probably, if Mr. Kaye had known him personally, he would not have formed so harsh a judgment on such little evidence. I can recall instances, within my own knowledge when Advocate-General, of Lord Dalhousie's indignation when acts of oppression and torture had attracted his notice in the public prints, and of his readiness to protect the native population from the recurrence of such acts. And I am sure that no one who was present on the Maidaun of Calcutta on the evening when Lord Dalhousie embarked, who saw the whole population moved, as one man, with a deep sense of regret and admiration, and observed the emotion of the departing statesman under the manifestation of that feeling, would consider him as one incapable of either exciting, or feeling sympathy. Many who witnessed that triumphant departure, had a melancholy foreboding that the curtain was falling on the last act of a great public career; that neither plaudits in India, nor well-merited honours at home, could avail to prolong a life almost exhausted in the public service. Others, more sanguine, hoped that he would recover his wasted strength, and enter on a new course of honour and success, as bright and glorious as his Indian career. But no one in that vast assemblage dreamed, that in a few years, the great reputation of their departing Governor would be doubted, sneered at, and assailed, or that it would ever be necessary to defend an administration that had been one brilliant and uninterrupted success.

LONDON:
PRINTED BY SMITH, ELDER AND CO.,
OLD BAILEY, E.C.

www.ingramcontent.com/pod-product-compliance
Lightning Source LLC
Chambersburg PA
CBHW031111020726
47495CB00007B/2147